GREGORY J. LAUGHERY

LIVING SPIRITUAL RHYTHMS

BOOK 2

destinēe

© 2013 Gregory J. Laughery

Without limiting the rights under copyright reserved above, no part of this publication may be reproduced, stored in, or introduced into a retrieval system, or transmitted in any form or by any means (electronic, mechanical, photocopying, or otherwise), without the prior written permission from the publisher, except where permitted by law, and except in the case of brief quotations embodied in critical articles and reviews. For information, write: info@destinee.ch

Reasonable care has been taken to trace original sources and copyright holders for any quotations appearing in this book. Should any attribution be found to be incorrect or incomplete, the publisher welcomes written documentation supporting the correction for subsequent printing.

Some Scripture quotations are taken from the Holy Bible, New International Version®. NIV®. Copyright ©1973, 1978, 1984 by International Bible Society.
Used by permission of Zondervan. All rights reserved.
Other Scripture quotations are taken from New Revised Standard Version of the Bible, copyright © 1989 by the Division of Christian Education of the National Council of the Churches of Christ in the USA. Used by permission. All rights reserved.

Published by Destinée Media, www.destineemedia.com
SECOND EDITION
Book formatting by Robynn Sims and Eric Reynolds
Cover design by Eric Reynolds
Copy editing by Robynn Sims
All rights reserved by the author.

ISBN 978-1-938367-14-4

CONTENTS

iv acknowledgments
v foreword

Dear Reader
vi

1 living spirituality

20 redemptive perspective

41 compassionate community

52 diverse reflections

acknowledgements

I am deeply grateful to Robynn Sims for her help with this book. In every way, she has made the book much better by far, than it was to begin with.

I owe a debt of gratitude to Eric Reynolds who always gave gracious and skilled assistance. He creatively accomplished all he was asked to do and plenty more.

Were it not for the staff, helpers, students, guest speakers, authors, poets, and blog commentators, who in some sense all make up the Swiss L'Abri community, there would be little to write.

Un grand Merci goes to each and every one.

foreword

Often we find ourselves questioning why our lives do not reflect what we believe. If we believe that Jesus was who he said he was, then why are we not living out the compassionate calling that he gave us? In a time when the words "daily devotional" mean little more than reading a single verse of the Bible attached to a simplistic personal application for the day, an indulgence all too frequently far removed from the totality of what God intends, Dr. Gregory J. Laughery offers us a fresh perspective. By intertwining language that is both provocative and engaging, he encourages us to use our imaginations and to begin to open our minds and our hearts to new ways of seeing, being, and living for the sake of the gospel, which truly is good news for all. As we do so, the hope is that these new ways of viewing the world, culture, Scripture, God, the church, and redemption will draw us back to the story that is of old—the story of God's love and truth. May you find yourself challenged and refreshed by Dr. Laughery's reflections, which are truly embodied in one who lives out his spirituality in humility and grace day after day.

Robynn Sims
Swiss L'Abri

Dear Reader,

Faced with so many false options and outlooks today, sunrise and sunset seem to close us into diminishing possibilities for finding realistic and true spiritual rhythms of life. The purpose of this book is to open up new horizons for living spirituality; for being in community with God, through Jesus Christ, in the power of the Spirit, and for living this intimate and profound reality out into the world in redemptive and loving ways.

Living Spiritual Rhythms has its focus on "living" as both verb and adjective. These rhythms therefore are living in the sense that they come out of my experience of being in community with God, and they are offered to you to be lived in an adventurous dynamic sense that I hope resonates with your own spiritual journey.

I want to extend to you dear reader, a warm invitation to deeply engage with this text. Keep it at hand, in your backpack or by your bedside, on a walk in the mountains or through the city. Meditate on the words, answer the questions, and take notes in the blank spaces and pages or in the margins. I've intentionally left plenty of room here for your responses and reflections. As you ponder the call to love and truth in this book, it is crucial to realize that we don't just read texts; they read us, as well. The goal of an encounter with this text is not to casually read through it, but to be read by it. In attentive reading and being read, there is an important moment of critical surrender that leads on to an appropriating of that which is not our own. Reading wisely opens us up to new possibilities. Being read challenges our hearts and minds, shapes our characters and identities, and changes our spiritualities and lives.

To be sure, we desperately need to be read by the text if we are to become better readers, and being better readers will help us discover more about spiritual rhythms of life for today.

living spirituality

"Living Spirituality" is the title of one of Dr. Laughery's books, and it is also the name of his blog. This concept of living is deeply ingrained in the life of the Swiss L'Abri community. Life is more than just getting by or making it up as we go along. True spirituality is living spirituality. Living spirituality is both adjective and verb. That is, this spirituality is living in that it originates in the living God, and then comes to us through creation, Scripture, Christ, and Spirit. It is also to be lived because it offers us the only true way to life in the midst of the pandemic of death.

The life, death, and resurrection of Christ are the imprint for redemption, which stamps itself upon us in living spirituality. These events are the key markers on the map for our journey and they open up the path to life. To obey from the heart is to live a new life, understanding the double-edged truth that grace reigns and that sin is no longer our master.

**From Ecclesiastical Sketches, 1822, Mutability
by William Wordsworth**

*From low to high doth dissolution climb,
And sink from high to low, along a scale
Of awful notes, whose concord shall not fail;
A musical but melancholy chime,
Which they can hear who meddle not with crime,
Nor avarice, nor over-anxious care.
Truth fails not; but her outward forms that bear
The longest date do melt like frosty rime,
That in the morning whitened hill and plain
And is no more; drop like the tower sublime
Of yesterday, which royally did wear
His crown of weeds, but could not even sustain
Some casual shout that broke the silent air,
Or the unimaginable touch of Time.*

Criticism is a necessary part of living spirituality, yet it is never to become an end in and of itself. If we have been naïve and believed the wrong things about God, ourselves, and others, there is indeed a place for criticism. The danger is that this criticism often turns into the whole story, blinding us to the relevance of trust and truth. But deep down there is a longing and wish to be called again, that is, called out of criticism and into community. It is crucial therefore to move past criticism. However, we want to do so without losing its insights and values as we are renewed in a critical trust and the true spiritual life in Christ.

This is slightly edited from a reader of the Living Spirituality Blog:
"I look at Scripture and see a gospel of grace, see how counter-cultural and even counter-intuitive almost everything godly can be. And then I hear about bailouts and entitlements and the rhetoric of political candidates and, frankly, the rhetoric of my family, and everything is contradictory and crazy. I'm struggling to figure out where to even begin separating what is good government and what is good Christianity. For example, the ethic of caring for the poor is huge in Scripture, but it seems like government programs that seek to do so are largely counter productive. So does a person vote by what could be considered a 'theological good' or by what seems most pragmatic?"

Fear rolls over us like the pounding waves of the sea.
This powerful emotion paralyses, blinds, controls, and in other ways disables us from being able to love God and others. Overcoming fear will lead us away from a self-centered life and turn us towards the foot of the cross of Christ, which will give us a new vision of ourselves, others, and the true meaning of love.

How do we evaluate what is true?

So much false guilt and shame weigh us down. True guilt confessed doesn't lead us to shame, but to renewal – the state of "no condemnation in Christ Jesus" leads to freedom.

What's the best way to deal with a shame-based identity?

False guilt and shame hang around our necks like heavy tombstones. Spiritual adultery lamentably takes many forms of convoluted expression in our times, from a neglect of the arts, to requiring similar hairstyles and dress. Real guilt confessed doesn't lead us to shame, but to renewal. These indeed must be days of insurrection. Spirituality, as being in community with God, is not found in the graveyard of deceptive options, which identify the dead, not the living. Followers of the crucified and risen One are alive, captured by the personage of him who embodies the way, the truth, and the life—they have broken out of the garden of death.

New Spiritualities

There has recently been a flourishing of new spiritualities. An Oprah worldview is a case in point: Hundreds of thousands of people are said to be following her views of spirituality and God. Is it so? Here's a brief summary of what she says:

1) It is mistaken to think that there is one way to God – there are many paths.
2) We need to open our minds to the indescribable.
3) If God's a jealous God, then God can't be God as this doesn't feel right to Oprah – because God is love.
4) God is not something to believe – God is. God is a feeling experience, not a believing one.
5) If it's about belief, it's not about God.

Depending on one's definition of spirituality, Oprah's point of view may be spiritual, but an important question is this: Does it lead us towards life or death?

Spirituality abounds in our world today. There is a syncristic tendency to blend aspects of culture, aspects of other religions, and aspects of tradition with our chosen faith. There must be a referent for our faith; something outside our experiences and outside our own selves that is what we are able to compare our living with. Jesus is that standard. As we seek to live spirituality in a way that is faithful to Scripture, we must also be willing to engage in dialogue with others. Living spirituality is both verb and adjective. Our spirituality is alive as we choose day by day to bring our decisions into the light of the true Referent.

FAR TOO OFTEN WE'RE OVERLY CONCERNED ABOUT WHETHER OR NOT OTHERS THINK HIGHLY OF US. BUT WHO DOESN'T WANT TO BE WELL LIKED AND APPRECIATED? THERE'S NOTHING WRONG WITH THIS WITHIN LIMITS OR DEGREES. AFTER ALL, IT'S A NORMAL PART OF BEING A HUMAN BEING. PROBLEM IS THAT LIMITS OR DEGREES ARE LAMENTABLY SURPASSED. WHAT EXTENT DO WE GO TO BE LIKED? WHAT I MEAN IS THIS: WHEN WE TAKE EVERY OPPORTUNITY TO BUILD OURSELVES UP, TO APPEAR SPIRITUAL, AND INSURE THAT WE WILL BE ACCEPTED, WE'RE OVERDOING IT AND MOVING WELL PAST NORMAL LIMITS OR DEGREES. FOLLOWING IN THE FOOTSTEPS OF JESUS WILL FREE US FROM THE TENDENCY TO SURPASS THE NORMAL. WHEN WE'RE ON THIS PATH, WE FIND OUT THAT BEING LIKED AND ACCEPTED HAS TO FIT IN WITH WHO WE ARE, NOT WHAT OTHERS MAKE US OUT TO BE.

OUR CHURCHES, ORGANIZATIONS, WORKS, AND ASSOCIATIONS EXIST TO BRING PRAISE TO GOD AND TO JOIN IN HIS WORK OF MISSION AND RENEWAL. THE CHILLING PREDICTIONS THAT CHRISTIANITY IN THE WEST IS IN SERIOUS TROUBLE MAY TURN OUT TO BE A TIMELY WARNING. WE ARE IN NEED OF A REVIVED SENSE OF PURPOSE – WHAT ARE WE DOING FOR THE POOR, FOR THE HUNGRY, FOR THE LOST, IN OUR NEIGHBORHOODS, OUR CITIES, OR ON THE OTHER SIDE OF THE WORLD? THINKING RIGHT THOUGHTS IS NOT ENOUGH. SAYING THE RIGHT THINGS IS INSUFFICIENT. GOD CALLS US TO ACTION IN SERVING OTHERS, SHOWING HOSPITALITY, AND SHARING GENEROUSLY. MAY OUR THOUGHTS, WORDS, AND ACTIONS BE SATURATED WITH GRACE AND THE LOVE OF CHRIST AS WE HUMBLY SERVE HIM.

HOW DO YOU DISCERN GOD'S WILL FOR YOUR LIFE?

Surpassing Surplus | *Our culture of surplus is exploding. Corrupt politicians, economic scandals, and greedy financial advisors may end up having done us a favor. Their duplicity and dishonesty should be a wake up call that critiques our consuming addictions. The shocking events of the economic crisis of 2008 and 2009 are appalling and terrible, but it's time to learn from them. We've journeyed so far from reality that we don't know where to find it anymore.*

We have to move in new directions of truth and integrity, with God at the center, Christ as mediator, and the Spirit, Scripture, and creation as our guides. That is, we have to follow in the footsteps of Christ in rejecting the life of progress and plenty as our goals, while we embrace the life of service and sacrifice, which finds its destiny in the cross and resurrection.

If we are Christians we are promised peace with God, but this doesn't necessarily translate into a peaceful and easy life. Looking for peace, tranquility, and less stress? Living spirituality, following the crucified and risen One in the present, does not mean that all our problems will be solved, but it does enable us to live in community with God in spite of them. Christian truth offers us an engagement with reality, not an escape.

Is it so?

Life is not complete,
truth is not complete,
and love is not complete.

Sometimes the conclusion drawn from these realities is that what we have now is just so, so. The future focus here, while correct, is too pessimistic about the present. That is, it is too not yet oriented and therefore consistently lamenting our lacks, rather than celebrating what's already possible in the present. Real life, real truth, and real love are all present possibilities and though each will never be complete now, they can already be part of the more of a future "how much more" and hence be sufficiently God, self, and other full to the limit. To be able to experience more than this will require a holistic transformation via death, which will then allow us to withstand the searing intensity of the Other; the presence of God—

life,
truth,
and love in completion.

*Take some time this week to read and study Romans 6.
This is an **amazing** chapter.
Of course, if you're able to, reading chapters
5, 7, and 8
would be helpful in order to understand
chapter 6
in its wider context.
Here are a few highlights for us from beginning to end in
this wonderful chapter:*

*__grace__ reigns and sin matters,
baptized into Christ's death to live a new life,
unity with Christ,
freed from sin,
Christ dies to sin once for all and lives to God,
consider yourself dead to sin and alive to God,
sin shall not be your master,
under **grace** not law,
free from sin and slaves to righteousness,
free from sin and slaves to God,
grace reigns and sin matters,
grace leads to life,
and sin to death.*

Fighting against the religious elite is a necessary element in following in the footsteps of Jesus. As Jesus armed himself against hypocrisy and trickery, he practiced a hermeneutics of suspicion that detected aims to undermine his new perspectives. Disciples should be alert to such attempts in their present context and carry around the sword of criticism. While critical insight is essential, we have to keep in mind that it is never an end in and of itself. The most important commandments, according to Jesus, are to love God with all you have, and your neighbor as yourself (Mark 12). All too often the sword of criticism, valid as it is, has to be put in the sheath of peace and love otherwise it ends up destroying those who wield it in Jesus'name.

As Christians we are called to be wise. "Ignorance is bliss" should be banned from church. Spirituality is deeply connected to thinking seriously about our faith and the world so that we might better reflect and represent the God we serve. Following the crucified and risen One is wisdom.

Panic in the stock markets.

The eyes of the world seem to be on wealth, when poverty remains one of our most significant and real problems. The homeless, starving, and destitute are ignored, while governments print money to shore up bankrupt and sometimes corrupt investors. If there is a time for renewal and a change of course, it is now. May God give us strength and wisdom to be living spirituality in these precarious times.

Giveness | *Situated in giveness is where we find ourselves. Giveness is under us, over us, and all around us. That which is given precedes ontology (human nature) and epistemology (human knowledge). Both these characteristics and features of humanity are second order discourse and neither is capable of being primary because they are already located in and preceded by the given. Take a moment to thank God for this truth that ultimately comes from him and testifies to him.*

One of the least attractive aspects of Christian spirituality may appear to be vulnerability. Protecting oneself and enhancing what one supposes ought to be safety, or is somehow owed to oneself, drives sensibilities like a massive wave crashing in the sea. Power is assumed to be found in shielding against all potential danger that might cause one to risk being vulnerable. True, risk may be present, though one ought not to see oneself as being slain by the sword of the victimizer, because vulnerability does not translate into being a victim, as it is real power and a strength that originates in love. Granted, the presence of such a vulnerability mode is dependent on who one is and where one is on the journey towards the ultimate destiny of facing God.

Have you ever reflected on the silence in heaven in Revelation 8? This occurs just after the opening of the seventh seal and before the sounding of the seven trumpets. A dramatic scene if there ever was one. Then an angel is given a massive amount of incense to offer with the prayers of the saints, which both arise to God. The prayers of the saints are important enough to God that there is silence, an awaiting the arrival of these prayers, and then action in response to them. After this the angel unleashes a series of natural warnings to highlight God's coming judgment. Prayer is important—vital—and does not take place in vain. God has created a world in which our prayers make a difference in the total outcome of his involvement in the world.

Why do you pray so often or so little?

Biblical Illiteracy | *Many of my students know very little about the Bible. Biblical illiteracy is growing at alarming rates, and this illiteracy inevitably leads to the impoverishment of the Christian faith and its ability to have an impact on culture for the sake of Christ. True and living spirituality is rapidly becoming lost to many people who don't have a clue as to how to read the Bible. To be people of the book means we have to be concerned about better and worse ways of reading and living what Scripture says.*

How can you improve your literacy?

When we experience oppression, suffering, and a sense of the absence of God in the Christian life, these experiences are not to be left unconnected or unrelated as if they stand on their own. Rather, we are to integrate these difficulties into the cross of Christ, which provides community and mediation. Christ shares our plight and reconciles our sorrows (in an "already, but not yet" context), and this is the lens through which we are to see our lives.

The "present" is never complete because it's always a present for me, and as it's for me, it will always be too small to be complete. Don't fight being finite and limited, but embrace it, and it will bring you closer to the truth.

(left intentionally blank for notes)

*Impoverished spirituality separates sacred and secular into ironclad compartments.
Living spirituality resists this unfortunate framing, stressing that it is crucial to realize that Christ is Lord of all of life and to live in the light of that truth.*

In living spirituality, Christians need to take time to nourish real relationships and to build communities that represent a shared life—a life together. We should learn to fast and feast as one, share books and stories jointly, listen to each other in attentive and caring ways, support and encourage each other, and be willing to accept and offer loving critique when necessary. Real relationships and shared lives, with Christ at the center and empowered by the Spirit, will lead to transformation into the image of Christ. We will experience new ways of seeing, being, speaking, and acting. And this type of transformation, lived in the Christian community, is also capable of being lived out in the world to the glory of God.

—From Living Spirituality: Illuminating the Path.

Our visual and audible destiny is set out for us, and in spite of the mystery of the present, we know where we're going, even though we lack clarity as to precisely how we'll be getting there.

Sometimes, unfortunately, Christians get the impression from a proof text reading of Scripture that to deny self or to lose self means to efface oneself. But this is not the case. Love of self is moral and biblical. A love for Creator and creation, for example, includes love of self, as it does love for the other. Love of self is essential for living spirituality, though it must never be the referent for itself.

The tragedy of monologue is that it impoverishes our spirituality. A one-dimensional perspective is ruinous for living spirituality as it robs us of what is really true. We are made by God to be in dialogue— God and self, self and others, others and world.

The Christian life is not whatever we make it to be, but seeking to live the sacred text in the space of the

gospel.

The itinerary of sense precedes us at any given moment in time as we gravitate towards the Father, Son, and Spirit who illumine the path ahead for all who have eyes to see and ears to hear.

Christian love in action is powerful and life-changing, but almost entirely absent in many Christian contexts. Let's face it. We are in desperate need of deep spiritual renewal. If we are to have a hand in reversing spiritual impoverishment today, it is essential to realize that there are no simple formulas, no superficial solutions, and no trite answers. Rather, we should be aiming for something like this: Through the power of the Spirit, we are to exemplify an informed, holistic, interactive, interpretive, theological, and redemptive spirituality that is lived in community with God. Christ's love is to flow through us and then out of us to each other, our neighbors, our enemies, all people, and the whole of creation. When this starts to happen, watch out—God is on the move and reversal is at hand.

Two Truths | Grace reigns and sin matters; *this statement captures the truth of living Christian spirituality. Because God has put into effect his rescue plan for humanity (and the planet) through fulfilling his covenant promise in Christ and through declaring us righteous, he calls us to live as his children in harmony as his family. Battered by sin, yet consoled by grace we have the gift of life to live now. Make the most of it today, while looking ahead to tomorrow with hope.*

In the novel The Kite Runner, *the main character's father is described as someone who was able to redeem himself because he chose to use his guilt and turn it into good. Redemption is not a specifically Christian idea, yet the explanatory power of its reality is deeply Christian. It seems as though in some ways, God has wired humanity in such a way that we desire redemption. This desire may not lead us to God, but there is a chance that our encounters with forgiveness, hope, and love will spark doubts in us that redemption is merely a human construct. And in those encounters, we may discover that though we desire to redeem ourselves, we cannot. Scripture speaks of redemption in the sense that slaves were "redeemed"; they were purchased so that they might have their freedom. Many perspectives are in dialogue as to how this redemption was initiated through the act of Christ's atonement. No matter where we fall on the spectrum of this theological point, we must acknowledge that redemption is a reality and that we are invited to not only accept the redemptive movement of God for ourselves, but to act out redemption in our own lives. The beauty of redemption as portrayed by Scripture is that not only is it meant for humanity, but for all of creation, and we are invited to join in this work.*

Having our life story re-narrated from a redemptive perspective won't make the sordid past go away, but it will provide us with a new way of looking at it and its capacity to negatively impact the present. Redeeming memories, through Christ and the power of the Spirit, is one of the ways we are brought into community with the God who lives. And in this community we are sheltered, comforted, and loved so that we in turn might shelter, comfort and love others.

Awaken us, oh God,

to the power of your forgiveness and grace so that we might experience your love and share this profound truth and reality with others. We often misunderstand or are misunderstood, and no one is innocent, although such a claim may be deceptively dear to our hearts. It's all too easy to make a mess of things. May your redemption, dear Lord, through the power of the Spirit, intensely slash into our lives and forever remind us that our sins are washed away in the blood of the crucified One. Please radically affirm in us our astounding directedness of being renewed day by day through the resurrected life of the risen One, as we move towards our ultimate destiny.

"I desire the joy of the Lord." We hear it all the time. Problem? Everybody wants it, but the statement is often nebulous as it tends to be rooted in personal experience or a feeling of the moment. While these are no doubt sometimes valid indicators of joy, they fall fleetingly short, and this is because they usually lack the theological force of the conviction. That is, the origin and source of the joy of the Lord, is the Lord, and what he has done, is doing and will do to redeem humanity and restore all things. When joy is rooted in the Lord, then it becomes more our own.

To walk in the newness of life is dramatically compared to the resurrection of Christ and is a metaphor for directing the whole of one's life toward the goal. And it is because Christ is raised that his followers are released, empowered, and challenged to live new lives in their present circumstances.

Oppressive regimes in church and society are appalling. Keeping laws, doing works of the law, and making busy-ness so frequently take precedence over God's redemption and love. People are reduced to management schemes and treated as commodities. New themes of redemption, community, and creativity need to be put in place that will challenge these awful tendencies and their attempt to rob people of knowing the God of truth and love.

Finding our way through the thicket of problems that perpetuate unbelief in God and the redeeming work of Christ is no easy task. And so often many churches are unhelpful in that they contribute to the production of unfaith by setting out views that have so little to do with truth and living in the world. To participate in the reversal of unfaith, our theology needs to be connected to, yet not dominated by, the world as we seek to be real and to live lives that have integrity, honesty, and a legitimate faith that can be discussed and be shown to make sense.

I recently talked to someone struggling with very low self-esteem. It turns out that she was measuring her worth by all kinds of false standards. She vainly tried to measure up, but continually failed. This caused unusually high levels of stress, anxiety, and eventually depression. Then, I asked her what connection her view of herself had with belief in God, and she confessed that she hadn't thought about this. The importance of a God connection and its ability to shed light on her life had been masked by self-deception, which is enticingly subtle, yet radically perverse. Being a believer in God and his offer of redemption in Christ are crucial for the whole of life generally, and for self-identity in particular. Don't forget to connect with God if you hope to find true standards of love, acceptance, and self-worth.

Jesus tells his disciples in John 14:1, "Do not let your hearts be troubled. Believe in God, believe also in me." **Today make it a point to affirm your belief in God and Jesus, and may your hearts not be troubled.**

To live a spirituality of the cross of Christ is to participate in the drama of God's creation and salvation. Let's follow in the footsteps of the crucified and risen One, be focused on the Scripture, and open to the Spirit as we are shaped by the dialogue of our community with God, each other, and the world. In the light of the power at work within us and our destiny to image Christ, may we rejoice and be thankful for this day.

When love has no basis or personal referent outside of ourselves—notably the Infinite One who is love—we are left to make it up as we go along. And as we attempt this fiction, there will be serious consequences. Love, when not anchored in and referring to the personal God, has limited significance and meaning. Love is not whatever we make it to be. Idealism and utopianism will be unsustainable, and a journey for the sake of the journey is a dead end—we need a destination, and the loving God provides that for us in Christ.

Real Resurrection | *The death of Christ is not the end of God's story. God's rule is further manifested in the resurrection. Christ was raised from the dead and is now present with God and interceding on behalf of his people. In much popular theology/spirituality today, the resurrection of Christ is reduced to the experience of Christ being raised in one's heart.*

Not only does such a perspective undervalue the map of Scripture and downplay a real theological referent for the heart, it leads back to the false referent of "me"—in fact, a form of dying spirituality. When there is no personal external referent for spirituality, notably the Infinite God, everything rests on "me" and my experience or feeling of Christ being raised. Such a "me" emphasis results in a naturalistic, human-istic referent stripped of any godly supernatural reality and power.

If Christ is merely raised in our hearts, our faith is in vain, and we have lost our view of the origin and ultimate source of spirituality, which first belongs to Father, Son, and Spirit, before it becomes our own.

Divine Blood | *Shedding animal blood was a pivotal part of sacrifice under the old covenant priesthood and it provisionally opened the way for God to have community with his people. But the blood of bulls and goats was never able to entirely deal with sin. There was a need for a greater sacrifice, and this need was met by Christ. As our great high priest, Christ is able to enter, once and for all, into the most holy place—the place where God dwells. The blood of the pre-existent, crucified and risen One, secures everlasting redemption. No repetition is necessary. He washes us—not with animal blood, which can never purify and cleanse—but with his own divine blood, which fully accomplished the covenantal requirements for decontamination. Christ sheds his blood on our behalf so that we too might enter into community with God and be wholly cleansed. This blood is of divine quality, and in its shedding there are divine consequences for our lives. With blood—the blood of Christ—the covenant is fulfilled, we are released from sin, we are justified, and we can begin to experience sanctification.*

Learning to imagine redemptively *is one of several key features that pertains to following Christ. As important as it is to realize that imagination is a crucial dimension of being human, it is all the more essential to begin to understand how necessary it is for belief in God and for living the Christian life. To imagine is not to make it up as we go along, but to be able to know God in a fuller way than we presently might, and to then live lives that reflect that fullness in Christ. Being more aware of the need to counter the rage of anti-God simulated images and the ideas connected to them will be an imaginative plus, as we begin to recognize that knowing God is a call to imagine God truthfully.*

There is a pathway to the truly spiritual life.
The gateway is Christ.
As we traverse the gateway onto the path,
we need to be more aware that the power
that is at work within us is that same
power that God exercised in Christ
when he raised him from the dead.
And that's an incredible and awesome power.

Redeeming and Renewing Church

Woe to churches and to those who lead them into distorting Christ's truth in word and deed.

Woe to churches and to those who lead them in refusing to forgive, in "playing God," and in seeking to condemn, rather than to offer Christ's redemption to others.

Woe to churches and to those who lead them in valuing money over and before God.

Woe to churches and to those who lead them into being like ravenous wolves in sheep's clothing, who terrorize God's flock with false teaching.

Woe to churches and to those who lead them into rejecting strangers and to only accepting people who look and act as they do.

Woe to churches and to those who lead them into shaming others.

Blessed are churches and those who lead them into God's truth.

Blessed are churches and those who lead them in repentance.

Blessed are churches and those who lead them in following Christ and the way of love.

Blessed are churches and those who lead them into mission for the sake of Christ.

Blessed are churches and those who lead them in showing hospitality to all in need.

Blessed are churches and those who lead them into redemption and forgiveness.

Blessed are churches and those who lead them into the journey of living spirituality.

Blessed are churches and those who lead them into humility.

Blessed are churches and those who lead them into serving others.

Blessed are churches and those who lead them to love God, love each other, and love all people.

Especially when Easter approaches each year and we prepare to be even more intentionally immersed in the death and resurrection of Christ, may this remarkable event weigh heavily upon us in new and refreshing ways. How grateful we are (and hopefully growing to be), that he inaugurated the Kingdom of God, brought salvation, is victorious over death through the resurrection, and opened the way into deep and everlasting community with God. On this basis, each of us can experience our own release from captivity in what Egypt represents: our own exodus, which will take us through the wilderness, Promised Land, and into a new heaven and new earth.

The Beauty of God | *Jeremy Begbie has written a number of fascinating and theologically astute books, including Resounding Truth. He also has an excellent essay in The Beauty of God: Theology and the Arts. In his chapter entitled "Created Beauty" he gives us six points to reflect on for understanding a theological account of beauty:*

> 1. *Beauty testifies to God's beauty in its own distinctive manner. Scripture shows us the Creator's faithfulness to the cosmos and his commitment to its otherness.*
> 2. *Beauty returns to Jesus Christ as the one in who creation has reached its goal.*
> 3. *Beauty revives a view of the Holy Spirit as the realizer of what Jesus Christ has achieved.*
> 4. *Beauty rejoices in diversity.*
> 5. *Beauty is cautious of a closed view of the world.*
> 6. *Beauty recognizes that beauty elicits desire – a desire to dwell in the beautiful. Beauty that glorifies God will evoke desire – a longing to explore and take pleasure in the beautiful.*

Beauty relates to God and his directedness towards revealing, incarnating, redeeming, renewing – a performance of beauty.

Money cannot save us.
Beauty cannot save us.
Poetry cannot save us.
Service cannot save us.

Only a suffering God,
a God of victims and victimizers,
a God who invites us to be true
and authentic selves beyond the
dark covering of insignificance,
can save us.

Dark Days in Europe | *Numerous European thinkers have proclaimed God is dead. People here tend to believe this unwarranted conclusion. In Switzerland, where I live, most of the massive cathedrals are empty and the local village churches are closing. A civilization without God will bring with it notable changes for generations to come. Social reform and the gospel have to be renewed as partners for the truth and for the good of Europe. If God is on our side, even in the darkest of times, some light will shine through that will have an impact and make a difference for the sake of Christ.*

Do you believe that Jesus' teachings in the gospels are a-political?

Deception and Destiny

One of the stark warnings in the biblical story is to be careful of self-deception. Be it from false prophets, false teachers, the religious elite, or ourselves, we have to reckon with the ever present danger of being deceived. Our sufficient, but now incomplete way through this dilemma, is the unending giveness of God in creation, revelation, Jesus Christ, the Spirit, and existence itself.

Finding the Way | *I remember several years ago having long discussions with a middle aged man and his wife who were traveling around the world searching for God. After some months passed, he said, "You know I thought I was a Christian, but now I realize that Christ may have been my savior, but he was never my Lord." He got it right. Seems like many of us hunger for a savior, yet we're not quite convinced we want to acknowledge Christ as Lord. This man came to understand the necessity of holding the two truths of the person and work of Christ together: he found God.*

The crucified and risen One is alive.
Christ is raised.
Celebrate the victory of life over death.

If you believe in Christ, how do you perceive having a white robe saturated in his blood, as portrayed in Revelation 7?

We who are Christians need not look to the consummation of God's rule with fear and trepidation. We too can shout, "HALLELUJAH!" for our Lord God Almighty reigns. Let us rejoice and be glad and give Him the glory.

Traces and piercings of the Holy Spirit mark us. The depth range of spirituality is a Spirit-fired transformation into the image of Christ. Bold redemptive actions in and through our lives, based on hope, bring about alignment with God and revelation of what God is doing in the world.

Theology cannot remain stuck in books and classrooms, but must become part of our own stories. Making truths our own is crucial, and there is nothing more vital for living spirituality than welcoming new and refreshing redemptive perspectives into our lives that will in turn be lived out for others.

How do we make something our own?

Life
often
appears
to be like a
flickering candle
flame dancing in the
texturally stark shadows of
nightfall's gentle breeze. Our dear
God, you know we're such delicately
crafted creatures, and that we long for your
lasting light. Burning to survive for another
day moves us towards our destiny—that final
meeting with piercing illumination where darkness
is extinguished and the light never ceases.
Resurrection and renewal, earth and body—
hope for life and light in the end to saturate
the whole of God's creation.

In what ways do you see yourself taking part in God's drama of redemption?

Empire versus Kingdom | *Empire-making moves in the direction of ideological madness and is addicted to arrogance, money, power, and possessions. For the church to follow in these destructive and ruinous footsteps is akin to suicide. Where is the rebellion against the status quo? Empire-building leaves people as casualties in its wake where bodies and hearts are crushed and strewn across the battlefield of dominance. Legalistic tirades and theological games, played at the highest level of manipulation and subterfuge aim to control the propagation of the ways things are. This is it, we hear, listen to us.*

For Christians there is another way. We should rebel against the unreal and stake our lives on loving people and embodying truth. We are called to hear and listen to God's word, not the propaganda of Empires. Christ came to deconstruct the Empire—both Caesar's and Satan's, bringing release to sinners in unleashing the Kingdom of God as further evidence of his rescue operation for the world.

Was Jesus of Nazareth an anarchist?

Oh God, we ask that you release us from the sin that enslaves and holds us captive to a woeful daily death.
Teach us the cadence of truth and life, so that we might serve you responsibly and in love. Mark us with your Spirit and show us the way to missionally, authentically, and effectively testify to your love as expressed in the lordship of Christ over the whole of life.

compassionate ***community***

---

*In cultures where the idea of "community" is
simply passed around like a commodity, and
often therefore ambiguous in its meaning,
the community of Christ is to be the
place where love and grace abound.
Those who do not believe will
be able to see who Christ is
and who Christians are
when they can see
the love that these
followers of Christ
have for each other
and all people.
When love
freely flows
in communities
that are living
the Kingdom of God
through an "economy of gift,"
love will overflow into a hurting world
desperate for forgiveness, redemption, and
reconciliation, which are the real currencies of*

God's Kingdom.

Being in **community** *with God and each other is a joy and a privilege. In seeking to do the Lord's work in the Lord's way, the apostle Paul urged us to have a deep* **unity** *amongst ourselves as we follow Christ, so that we might glorify God with one heart and voice. To accept one another then, just as Christ has* **accepted** *us, will ultimately be pleasing to God. As we are bound together in our various callings, let's continue to focus on our* **purpose** *to serve God wherever we are and in whatever we're doing. It's all too easy to lose our way as we face threats and are exposed to the fears of a world spinning off into chaos. God is* **faithful***; therefore, do not be faint of heart.*

Pray today especially for our sisters and brothers that face torture, rape, kidnapping, and other forms of persecution.

Living in community brings with it a unique set of rhythms of life. My story involves being part of a Christian community for over twenty years.

Here are a few remarks on spiritual illumination.

Spirituality is not less than words, although it may rightly be far more. Poetry, prayer, and prose target communion.

Let's think, feel, imagine, and experience spirituality as it revolves through a dynamic motion that is in dialogue with God, Scripture, the world, and others.

There is nothing static about this community, and attempting to find a pleasant comfortable balance is often closer to ignorance, than to wisdom.

*Meditate on these three.
They are crucial, and should be
having a profound impact in our
lives for the sake of Christ.*

- *We believe that the arts and cultural participation are vital.*

- *We believe in church as community, as a Scripture reading community, and as a living community.*

- *We believe in hospitality and compassionately welcoming strangers.*

May our lives reflect and embody
the redemptive power of Christ as we seek to
show mercy and love to each other.

Welcoming strangers *into homes and churches is a lost art—it's called hospitality. This loss strikes at the heart of Christianity, which all too often these days is seen to be inverted and self-serving. Jesus was concerned with hospitality and providing shelter to those who were outcasts. As his followers, we dare not at least do the same.*

If Christianity is true, why is there so little hospitality in so many churches?

Christ stands at the door and calls, awaiting a response from anyone who hears his voice. This picture of the crucified and risen One standing at the door is not a threat, but a promise. There he is, and he is calling out. No doubt this imagery should jolt and challenge us. Whenever we hear his voice, it is time to open the door. He assures us that our hospitality will not be deceptively abused.

Be open to forgiving and loving. Compassionate community is a tremendous apologetic and a living testimony to Christ.

Beyond memory and imagination God reveals in word and world. In spite of the immemorial and the impossible, God speaks and acts in creational and salvific ways for himself and for us. He loves us lovingly, discloses himself sufficiently, and wants us to know through faith that he is there. The offer, invitation if you will, is to be in community with the only God who is.

The setting of hospitable boundaries is crucial, not for the purpose of keeping others out, but so that they may be invited in. In so doing they then receive and experience a life-giving hospitality, centered more in love than in duty.

Terrestrial everyday life is made up of our waking and sleeping, eating and resting, going out and coming in, working and playing. Sharing hardship and joy, success and failure, birth and death, traces our lives with fine and delicate lines, which give us character and pierce into the marrow of our existence. Being in community with God and each other is an everyday affair, not a once a week ritual. In the spiritual rhythms of life today, we are challenged to open the door to God consciousness in that which we think, feel, do, and say, as we go through and participate in all the activities that shape and contribute to our walking moment by moment through life together.

There is a central and wonderful tension in living spirituality:
Grace reigns and sin matters.
Now, let's live this truth in community with God and each other.

Despite the many obstacles and false paths we take,
Jesus says he is the way, the truth, and the life.
Follow him and find community with God.
Reflect on what it means to be in community with God.

Searching for Space | *It seems to me that our culture is increasingly one of dislocation and fragmentation. Modernist notions of stability and permanence are rightly being shattered. But in their place postmodern nomads now wander from here to there—to nowhere. And this meandering is not merely a physical or geographical phenomenon, as it is perceived in many who appear to have ultra-low levels of concentration and hyper-deficient attention spans. No homes. No boundaries. No limits – wandering into a never ending journey. All these powerful delusions leave us destitute and floundering. We long for the real, but it seems so unattainable and out of reach. Wandering around like nomads without homes, we continue our search for the authentic, hoping that someone, somewhere, or something has credibility. We all desperately need a place to dwell, but we need also to recognize that this space, for now, is both already and not yet.*

In a day when that which is said to be
Christian
*often produces unfaith,
what kinds of Christian witness
might lead people towards faith
in God and the saving work of Christ?*

When we are facing troubled times, the apostle Peter reminds us as aliens and exiles to live in a way that is pleasing to God. We are to love one another with tender hearts and humble minds. Above all, in 1 Peter 4:8-9 he proclaims, love each other deeply, because love covers over a multitude of sins. Being in community with God should ripple out into compassionate community with each other.

Love is not making it up as we go along. God is love and therefore God gives us direction as to what love is. Love is never less than justice, but always more. And superabundantly more. The path of love is kind, gentle, and gracious. It doesn't cherish keeping a list of grievances, but neither is it unchallenging. Christians are to love God, each other, and all human beings, as we seek to be those who demonstrate the truth that God sent Christ to redeem and restore the world.

Love & Justice | *Humanness in its fullest polyphonic sense is deeply connected to being in community with God and others. Love and justice are to characterize this community. Perceiving and doing truth are to shatter and debunk false ideologies that imprison the disenfranchised and unloved. Feeding the poor and loving the rejected challenge us to mark out a clear path that shows our embodied love for God and a concern for bringing justice to an unjust world.*

Where do love and justice become actualities in your life?

Loving someone so much that you give them the freedom to not love you in return may be the closest we ever come to divine love.

Giving up power, giving up control, and portraying ourselves to be better than we are can be heavy burdens to release. These tendencies are so deeply ingrained in us, and to a large extent identify who we are. The radical need to replace them with love, compassion, and grace is all too evident. Where do we start? Seeking to follow in the footsteps of Christ is a beginning. And we are called to make efforts to go against these tendencies through learning new ways of living and of being spiritual people, which promotes transformation in ourselves and our communities as we await the future return of the Lord.

When cycles of fear and doubt surge in and through us, we need to try to be aware that we're not alone. God and others are with us and share in what we're working through. Thinking it's only us will alienate us and cause us to have a sense of isolation and disconnection from everyone else. True, those close to us may not have a clue, and I know that's hard. In these circumstances, however, it is crucial to recognize and remember that we're also part of a non-geographical global community of believers, many of whom do understand us and share our plight as we long for renewal, practice hope, and search for God.

Disconnected and reoriented | *Unplugged is not just a term for an MTV acoustic concert, but it can be a metaphor for a life connected to people. When we're constantly plugged into devices we deprive others and the possibility of a two way interaction is broken. We don't receive from them, nor can we give to them. We've lost the way. There's enough dehumanization around. Unplug, at least for a substantial part of your life, and live.*

Become a g-local Christian. *Those who follow in the footsteps of Christ are called to a global and a local community and are to have an intense passion and concern for both spheres of life in the body of Christ. Keep the fires of love, trust, community, and compassion burning for brothers and sisters wherever they are found.*

Christians should be *in the front line when it comes to preserving people and the environment. Caring for the poor is a command that deserves our whole-hearted participation, and our concern for the eco-systems of the natural world is not only an expression of a stewardship of creation, but of our love for others.*

Christian parents *all too often provide an atmosphere of inauthenticity and legalism which, among other things, results in a failure to align saying and doing. Children see this incongruity and, because of it, end up rejecting the faith that it is supposedly based on. When a more real expression of Christ comes their way, instead of finding their previous observations reinforced, they discover that they are challenged. Good! This frequently leads to a renewed faith and an authentic embrace of Christianity that parents sometimes unfortunately reject because it is a faith that is not like theirs. Not good! If you're a parent reading this—be open to a reformulated faith in Christ on behalf of your children. If you're a child reading this—don't give up on pursing a true faith or the hope that your parents will become more open to where you stand as a Christian.*

Signals that the Western Christian church is in serious decline are all around us. Here in Europe, the massive cathedrals in most major cities are empty. In America people are bailing out of their churches in droves. Australia and New Zealand face similar scenarios. Now is the time to return to Christ and the Scriptures and to pray that God would renew his people in community. Pray that he would instill in us all a redemptive, missional, and loving spirit that will be graciously lived out into the world. **There is a mass exodus from traditional churches going on. What are you doing? Staying in? – getting out?**

diverse reflections

Reading Scripture
Real Grace - II Corinthians 8
II Corinthians 8:1-15
Needing Grace and Living Grace
Living Righteousness
Unequally Yoked? (II Corinthians 6:1-7:1)
Imagination
Reading Culture
Christian Idolatry
A Letter and A Response
Depth in Spirituality
Passage from John 3
Text and Worship
Memories
To Christian Parents (a letter)

Tension and the Kingdom of God
Fairy Tales: A New Beginning?
Expectations from God
Misunderstanding the Holy Spirit
Mark's Prologue
Biblical Interpretation
Destiny
And Rome Fell – Rev. 18
Poetic Spirituality
ME
Proverbs 13:10-14
Flight from the Ordinary
The Shroud of Secrecy
False Absolutes
Looking Towards Home

Reading Scripture | *One of my suggestions for reading Scripture is that we develop wise and Spirit-fired reading habits. I think we need to be more intentional about being actively aware of the significant dangers of misreading the text in order to allow ourselves to be read by it. Spirit-powered efforts to counter misreading, combined with more informed readings, will help transform our communities and churches. This more faithful and fittingly inspired embodiment of Scripture can then be lived out in the world. The magnitude of this embodiment could have a profound impact on highlighting and affirming God's missional purposes in reconciling the world to himself in Christ.*

Real Grace: 2 Corinthians | *This letter is one of my favorites. I fear it all too often falls under the shadow of 1 Corinthians and as a result we miss its thought provoking and action oriented illumination. In chapters 1-7 readers have received another glimpse into the complex context of Paul and the Corinthians, and the theological and personal concerns related to it. Hopefully, this perspective helps us to better understand the letter and the real gems that it offers us. Before turning to explore chapter 8 in more detail, let me just point you to a few of these:*

1) *Conflict in relationships is a reality. How to view the other is important, especially in the Christian community—the truth of the gospel is at stake.*

2) *Struggles and difficulties in our lives are not ends in and of themselves. God is the God of all comfort.*

3) *Dangers of bringing the truth of the gospel into question should cause us to reflect carefully on our actions.*

4) *Godly grief leads to repentance and repentance leads to salvation and salvation to God. Salvation and God are the referents of repentance, which lead us into community with God and each other.*

5) *God is at work in our lives, and this knowledge should make us aware of many things, including the importance of justice.*

6) *Where do our own loyalties lie? How are we to practice a hermeneutics of trust and suspicion in life-giving ways that represent the gospel?*

On the next page you'll find a part of the text I'd like you to consider being read by. Read it carefully, and if you have time, read the whole letter, in order to be better read and to discover more about real grace.

2 Corinthians 8: 1-15

1 And now, brothers and sisters, we want you to know about the grace that God has given the Macedonian churches. 2 Out of the most severe affliction, their overflowing joy and their extreme poverty welled up in rich generosity. 3 For I testify that they gave as much as they were able, and even beyond their ability. Entirely on their own, 4 they urgently pleaded with us for the privilege of sharing in this service to the saints. 5 And they did not do as we expected, but they gave themselves first to the Lord and then to us in keeping with God's will. 6 So we urged Titus, since he had earlier made a beginning, to bring also to completion this act of grace on your part. 7 But just as you excel in everything—in faith, in speech, in knowledge, in complete earnestness and in your love for us—see that you also excel in this grace of giving. 8 I am not commanding you, but I want to test the sincerity of your love by comparing it with the earnestness of others. 9 For you know the grace of our Lord Jesus Christ that though he was rich, yet for your sakes he became poor, so that you through his poverty might become rich. 10 And here is my advice about what is best for you in this matter: Last year you were the first not only to give but also to have the desire to do so. 11 Now finish the work, so that your eager willingness to do it may be matched by your completion of it, according to your means. 12 For if the willingness is there, the gift is acceptable according to what one has, not according to what he does not have. 13 Our desire is not that others might be relieved while you are hard pressed, but that there might be equality. 14 At the present time your plenty will supply what they need, so that in turn their plenty will supply what you need. Then there will be equality, 15 as it is written: "He who gathered much did not have too much, and he who gathered little did not have too little."

Being Generous: 2 Corinthians 8:1-7 | *In chapter 8, Paul is going to revisit, via Macedonia, the matter of the collection for the Jerusalem church, which he already mentioned back in 1 Corinthians 16. This collection had been initiated, but not yet completed; therefore, he wants to raise the subject again in anticipation of the return of Titus to Corinth. However, this is not Paul's only concern here in this letter. He also targets the centrality of grace, and gives it a careful exposition in chapters 8-9.*

We enter new territory in verse 1. Paul initially wants his readers to know something of the grace of God toward the Macedonian churches. This grace relates, as verse 2 points out, to overflowing joy in the midst of affliction and the riches of their focused generosity. Normally, Paul uses the more specific word "charis" or "charisma" for a gifting or grace of this type, which is often connected with something received, but here he refers to overflowing joy and overflowing generosity. God's grace has been given, and in Paul's context, continues to be given, which results in an overflowing joy and in the Macedonians' unprecedented generosity. Perhaps this quite unusual concept—the reciprocity of grace received and generosity given—is something we would do well to think more about. Could it be that there is a place for God's grace to us being revealed through our grace; in this case, our generosity to the other?

Notice the context of the Macedonian churches, which Paul no doubt uses to serve as an example to the Corinthian church. Their generosity is shown in the midst of severe affliction, which may have been due to Roman possession of their land and material wealth. Yet, out of overflowing joy and the depth of their poverty they were able to manifest God's grace. It is likely that in comparison to the Corinthian church, the Macedonian churches were fairly poor. But what counts for the apostle here is their attitude and spirit, not necessarily the quantity of what is offered.

This is explained in verses 3-4. The apostle writes that these Christians have given far beyond their own ability, and they have given in an unsolicited manner. God's grace in these churches is manifested in their sacrificial care for the other. Not only in their case was this sacrifice not requested, but they actually appealed to have the privilege of participating in a collection for the saints in Jerusalem who were more poverty stricken than themselves.

The Macedonians' giving went far beyond expectation, as verse 5 goes on to point out. It originated and culminated in a giving of themselves to the Lord and also a giving of themselves to the apostle through God's will. Perhaps Paul has at least two points here. First, he is aiming to defuse any Corinthian plot in regard to the accusation that he is only after their money. Second, he is implying that the Macedonian churches recognized his God-given apostleship and authority, both of which are validated in his serving others for Jesus' sake (4:5).

In verse 6 Paul moves more directly to the matter at hand. Titus will return to Corinth. As a result of the unanticipated interest in the collection by the Macedonian churches Titus is going to seek to bring the "act of grace" which had begun in Corinth to its completion.

With verse 7, Paul draws this section to a close. He directly challenges the church in Corinth to bring to completion the grace of giving, which in this specific case is the collection for the impoverished in Jerusalem. As the church in Corinth was known for its manifestation of certain other spiritual gifts, Paul here picks up the verb "overflow" from verse 2 and lists a number of graces the Corinthians do overflow in. If this is the case, should they not also overflow in the grace of giving?

The church in Corinth may have had a problem with a focus on the other, perhaps both within and outside its own community context. No doubt there were strengths in the church, but this seems to be a glaring weakness, which may have been due to an insufficient understanding of grace. Grace is not only to be received for oneself, but it is to be given to the other.

Giving and Grace: 2 Corinthians 8:8-15 | *Paul's exhortation is quickly followed in verse 8 by a sort of disclaimer. He is not commanding this grace from the Corinthians, as it is unlikely that he had received any such command from the risen One. He rather wants to know where the level of their love stands with respect to that of the Macedonians.*

In this context, the apostle again returns to the wonderful reality of interchange, now expressed in verse 9. He has already written of this back in 5:21. No doubt the aim here with this use of metaphors is to heighten and sharpen the understanding of grace, while also addressing the matter at hand. But how does this work out? The model of grace that the Corinthians know of is the Lord Jesus Christ. What they may not have realized is the analogy between this grace and the grace of giving to others. As Christ has become something that he is not so that they might become something they are not, he takes their place in order that they might be graced with his. So too, grace has to do with not only receiving, but giving.

Perhaps this is a new configuration of grace for us. It may be appropriate to say it this way: Grace is for passing on, but we should stress that doing so must be rooted first in humble receiving. In other words, passing on grace is not merely based on performance, but on reception which is the referent for its being passed on. The life and work of Christ are other-focused so that those who receive it might move from being self-centered towards being Other- and others-centered. This other-centered capacity will, in turn, affirm the truth of the receivers being new selves. The perception of interchange then functions on at least two levels. First, Christ and only Christ can stand for us; the one who was rich becomes poor, so that others might receive grace. Second, those who receive this unique grace must then pass it on to another. Grace received is then refigured through grace given. As this grace has been given to them they should carefully consider the grace of giving to the other.

In verses 10-12, following the metaphorical power of verse 9, Paul moves into giving his advice to the Corinthians more directly. Remember, he has done a similar thing previously on another issue back in 1 Cor. 7. This advice is what he understands to be the most helpful for them. He looks back in time in order to remind the Corinthians that it would be most helpful for them if there was a greater symmetry between their wanting and their doing.

It is true that they were "not only" the first to start a collection for others, "but also" wanted to accomplish this offering. However, what had broken down was the doing part of the reality. The Corinthians wanted to initiate something, yet perhaps like many of us, the actual doing of this is where configured grace – the grace we've received never becomes refigured in our own lives before being passed on to the other. Wanting the right things is admirable; however, this commendable desire must reach the other in actual doing. The Corinthians' willingness, their voluntary response to a need was there, but this now must translate into action that accomplishes something in the world.

Notice that this completed action, from Paul's perspective, is related to the capacity of this church. They are being encouraged to go ahead and do what they said they would within the context of what is possible. What is most important here is the attitude of giving, which is in turn what makes it acceptable before God.

In verses 13-14, Paul shifts direction somewhat. With another explanatory "for" flowing from the assurance that he is not encouraging the Corinthian believer to give what he or she does not have, Paul anticipates another question or concern.

Would it be appropriate if the one profits at the other's expense? He is not suggesting, in this context, that some be in poverty, while the others are taking advantage. What he aims at is equality. But what does Paul have in mind here? Perhaps, in looking ahead, his point is that the Corinthians will receive the fellowship and prayers of the saints as 9:14 states, and that if circumstances were reversed, they also would benefit from aid of a similar type. Verse 15 brings the section to a close with a quote from Exodus 16:18. The principle in this passage is that those who had a considerable amount had none left over and those who had less had enough. As God was concerned with equality and generosity during Israel's wilderness period, Paul now stresses its ongoing relevance at the present time.

In conclusion to this exposition of II Corinthians 8:1-15 here are a few salient points to think more and better about, and act upon:

1) *It is essential for us to understand and live out the reality that God's grace expresses itself in both being received and also in being given. This expression is rooted in the grace of the Lord Jesus Christ and the reality of interchange between us and him, which takes place as a result of it. In turn this reality brings about an attitude of overflowing joy leading to the grace of generosity towards others. What kind of world makes this interchange possible? What kind of world makes it possible to give as much as one is able, even beyond one's ability? What kind of world allows one to overflow in the grace of giving and to actually do grace? The world of the biblical text is the only one that both configures these truths, while at the same time opening possibilities for us to take part in this world, and as we do so, to have our lives refigured through participating in receiving and giving God's grace.*

2) *Paul's advice is that there needs to be a greater symmetry between wanting and doing in the lives of Christians. A practical following through with grace is the one the piercing marks of a new self who participates in the interchange that the Lord Jesus Christ has brought about.*

3) *Equality in graces is to be an essential reality in the Christian community as it lives its faith out into the world.*

Needing Grace and Living Grace | *There is so much pressure to measure up to false standards, rules, and regimes. Freedom is always just around the corner, down the street, and in flight to somewhere else. God, we need your grace.*

All of us face notions of counterfeit guilt and shame, which hang around our necks like the massive crosses of stone that adorn our churches of iron and steel. We need God's grace.

In the midst of individual or community conflict where boundaries have been inappropriately violated, we have caused pain and hardship or received pain and hardship from others. God, we need your grace.

When we are mired in and weighed down by spiritual adultery, we need God's grace.

Huge inequalities exist between men and women that have resulted in ruinous oppression and social degradation, while racial hatred escalates and uses skin color fallaciously in attempts to describe humanness. God, we need your grace.

Some preachers have become rhetors seeking to cure us of all ills, so that our lives would be blessed and rewarded with windfalls of cash. We need God's grace.

Ridiculous divisions over petty and inconsequential issues characterize so many Christian lives. God, we need your grace.

Mission has been buried under a tombstone of self-preservation. We need God's grace.

And love? Whatever happened to love? God, we need your grace.

When it comes to grace, I wonder if it's usually thought of as something given by God and received by us. No doubt this is a profound truth, but it is often framed in this way: God gives, we receive – end of story. While God giving and we receiving grace is essential, I think we should see this as the beginning and not the end of the story. This may be a new way of configuring grace, but it is crucial.

Here's why: Remember, as we've previously seen a moment ago, the apostle Paul points this out in 2 Corinthians 8-9: received grace is to be passed on to others. He passionately shows his readers that grace is not merely to be experienced as passive, but is to be an action from those who have received it towards those in need. This is living grace as both verb and adjective. God's grace is living and it is to be lived. Quite simply—grace is giving to others for it to be fully grace. When there is an overflowing reception of grace, there should be an overflowing giving of grace. Grace is not a private matter, nor is it something to keep within the walls of our bodies, houses, churches or computers. If you're on the verge of giving grace to another, then go ahead—complete the action—release grace out into the world.

This grace of giving, it should be noted, is to take place in the context of freedom, which allows each to give according to their means. Paul will have none of the strong arm or calculated manipulating tactics that often identify so much of contemporary Christianity. There is a great deal of deception in today's world, and it can all tend to be about money, as so often money is at the heart of the deception.

Let's move in a new direction. Living grace, grace, and more grace. Giving grace is not to be done grudgingly, but out of a joy to help. God loves a cheerful giver because this is the attitude from which giving is to take place. There are no stipulations concerning quantity here. It doesn't matter. What's important is attitude—a living grace attitude.

The God of grace is able to make grace abound, so that we will abound in every good work. And we will be made rich in every way in order that in turn we might be generous to others and through this bring thanksgiving to God. His superabundant manifestation of grace should produce an abundant manifestation of grace, which will result in enlarging and increasing our harvest of righteousness. The key to unlock the door to all this is interchange: "For you know the grace of our Lord Jesus Christ, that even though he was rich, yet for your sakes he became poor so that you through his poverty might become rich" (II Corinthians 8:9).

Living Righteousness | *Carol was always busy in a flurry of activity. She did, and did to the point of exhaustion. What was behind it all? Why the stress and anxiety in her role as a Christian to do and do? Carol thought she needed to do so that God would declare her righteous. This required her constant performance for others and for God. She learned how to make herself appear to be a strong Christian, but she came to realize she was wearing a mask. She thought God should hide her sin—not because she was sorry for it, but so that she might look better before others and not be rejected.*

A powerful legalism flourished in Carol's life. Everything stood or fell on how well she followed the laws. If she thought she had done enough in a day, then she was entitled to see herself as worthy and meriting justification. If she didn't measure up to her codes and regimes, or those that others had imposed upon her, she viewed herself as condemned. This vicious circle led her to repeated defeat and perplexity, with seemingly no way out of the maze.

Carol needed to become aware of an entirely new way of seeing things. It was a revelation to her to understand that Christ did for her what she could never do for herself. And that she had misconstrued what she was asking God to do for her. God is not out to hide our sin, but to expose it. In Christ, God had already done everything necessary for her justification. If she confessed Christ as Messiah, she was justified. To be justified by God, to be declared righteous, was the gift she could accept with the empty hands of faith. Carol had been so caught up in a doing mentality that she missed the essential truth of justification as a gift. There is, of course, a place for a being-and-doing connection, but Carol had put doing before being a Christian.

Unequally Yoked? | *Let's explore reading a controversial text. Here's the text I'd like you to consider being read by. Read it carefully, and if you have time, read the whole letter, in order to be better read by it.*

2 Corinthians 6:1-7:1

¹ As God's fellow workers we urge you not to receive God's grace in vain. ² For he says,

"In the time of my favor I heard you,
and in the day of salvation I helped you."

I tell you, now is the time of God's favor, now is the day of salvation. ³ We put no stumbling block in anyone's path, so that our ministry will not be discredited. ⁴ Rather, as servants of God we commend ourselves in every way: in great endurance; in troubles, hardships and distresses; ⁵ in beatings, imprisonments and riots; in hard work, sleepless nights and hunger; ⁶ in purity, understanding, patience and kindness; in the Holy Spirit and in sincere love; ⁷ in truthful speech and in the power of God; with weapons of righteousness in the right hand and in the left; ⁸ through glory and dishonor, bad report and good report; genuine, yet regarded as impostors; ⁹ known, yet regarded as unknown; dying, and yet we live on; beaten, and yet not killed; ¹⁰ sorrowful, yet always rejoicing; poor, yet making many rich; having nothing, and yet possessing everything. ¹¹ We have spoken freely to you, Corinthians, and opened wide our hearts to you. ¹² We are not withholding our affection from you, but you are withholding yours from us. ¹³ *As a fair exchange—I speak as to my children—open wide your hearts also.*

¹⁴ *Do not be yoked together with unbelievers. For what do righteousness and wickedness have in common? Or what fellowship can light have with darkness?* ¹⁵ *What harmony is there between Christ and Belial? What does a believer have in common with an unbeliever?* ¹⁶ *What agreement is there between the temple of God and idols? For we are the temple of the living God. As God has said: "I will live with them and walk among them, and I will be their God, and they will be my people."*

¹⁷ *"Therefore come out from them*
 and be separate, says the Lord.
Touch no unclean thing,
 and I will receive you."

¹⁸ *"I will be a Father to you,*
 and you will be my sons and daughters, says the Lord Almighty."

^{7:1} *Since we have these promises, dear friends, let us purify ourselves from everything that contaminates body and spirit, perfecting holiness out of reverence for God.*

2 Corinthians 6:1-10 | *In the first section of chapter 6, Paul now moves on from those in Christ being a new creation, and the claim that God was reconciling the world to himself in Christ (5:11-21), to a more direct address to his readers in verses 1 and 2.*

Notice that the apostle has written (5:11-21) that he is an ambassador of Christ and it is as such that he implores the Corinthians to be reconciled to God. The gateway into community with God is Christ, and this is the first step, for us, in participating in God's gracious purpose to reconcile the world to himself. As it is so wonderfully put in 5:21, it is God who made him who had no sin to be sin for us, so that we become the righteousness of God. Imagine and reflect on that for a moment—being the righteousness of God in Christ is truly a marvel and a direct result of reconciliation. Righteousness, in this context, might be said to conflate the actions of love and justice—that hyper-delicate dialogue which situates the lives we live as Christians on a tightrope, where we have the marked tendency to fall off on one side or the other. God forgive us. Yet Christ is able to maintain the balance perfectly, and to do so with us on his shoulders. Paul is going to build on being ambassadors of Christ, the very thing that some in Corinth may have been suspicious of (read chapters 1-5), making an appeal in chapter 6. First of all it is pointed out in 6:1 that he is working together with God. Next, following on from 5:20, he appeals to his readers directly with "you."

The appeal is not to have received God's grace in vain. How might this be happening? Possibly, it was taking place in at least two ways: First, being lured away from the gospel by an imitation, perhaps something too focused on some form of external performance and not enough on inward change that brings forth a "real" and "transformative" modification of one's actions. Second, God's grace is likely, in this context, to be related to Paul working with God on behalf of the Corinthians. They are at risk of rejecting God's grace as it manifests itself in Paul's preaching of the gospel. To reject Paul's apostolic word is to entertain rejecting the gospel itself.

In verse 2, Paul cites Isaiah 49:8 and applies it to his present context. He announces that "now" is the time of salvation, and as such, there is a need to pay attention to God's reconciling activities that have been unleashed in Christ, and to not have received his grace in vain. God is a missional God who is reconciling the world to himself in Christ and no longer counting peoples' sins against them. This salvific trajectory has been set in motion, and Paul as an ambassador of Christ, longs for his readers to recognize God's saving purposes and to bring their actions into line with that which is happening "now" in salvation time.

In the next verses, 3-10, Paul writes of a number of troubles, nine of them; a number of graces, eight of them; and a number of antitheses, ten of them. This is another attempt to show that the new covenant ministry has not manipulated or defrauded anyone. No one has legitimate cause to stumble or turn away towards another gospel. On the contrary, Paul has done all he could to not be a target of criticism as this may have reflected on the apostolic ministry that was so central to the truth of what God was doing in Christ.

But what shall we do with verses 4b and following where the apostle launches into a double commendation. It is worth again remembering the literary context into which he writes. Is he now contradicting himself in regard to what he has already written in 3:1 and 5:12?

No doubt, as we have already seen, new covenant ambassadors and especially Paul's apostleship, as far as the Corinthians were concerned, was highly dubious and considerably suspect. There were those who saw his difficulties as inappropriate for one who claimed to be an apostle of the risen and glorified One. Paul, remember, is facing character criticism on the one hand and action criticism on the other. But we must recall that related to these forms of criticism, at least as Paul has it, is the danger of critiquing the gospel itself.

Into this context he now writes that it is possible to see the apostolic ministry being proclaimed by servants of God, which notice is not found in 3:1 or 5:12, in two equally commendable ways. A true apostle is commended for great endurance in the midst of adversity and for displaying the power of God in spite of dire circumstances. Paul was oppressed and opposed, but also faced more voluntary hardship because of the nature of his ministry moving him place to place so frequently and the choice not to burden others for his support.

Yet dealing with such adversity in great endurance is only part of the apostolic picture. Paul goes on in verse 6b to write that by the Spirit and the power of God he displays an unhypocritical love and he proclaims the word of truth in kindness and patience with understanding and integrity. In this context, the model of apostolic ministry is the crucified and risen One.

This goes on to further and is expressed in a number of "as if" and "yet" contrasts beginning in verse 8c. All of these could be said to mark apostolic ministry. The contrasts show what so often tends to be a human perspective (likely here to be that of the Corinthians), versus a godly one in regard to the apostolic mission.

.
..
...

Thoughts?

2 Corinthians 6:11-13 | *In the next three verses 11, 12 and 13, the suffering, yet victorious apostle again addresses the issue of his community with Corinthians directly. What he has proclaimed to them continues to speak. It is a saturated word that is not silenced. An open mouth also relates to an open heart. Paul's "open wide" heart is likely to refer to his community with the Corinthians, including his visits and his letters, as well as his present desire to fight to hold onto the relationship and make a future visit.*

Paul makes his affection for them clear, and that at the time of writing, the affection was not reciprocal. In spite of some of the accusations against him, he wants the Corinthians to know his feelings.

The apostle completes his thought with the appeal for fair exchange; one open-wide heart for another. He is still willing, still longing for a deep community with the Corinthians. As he is their father in the gospel, he addresses them as his children to again reinforce the relationship they already have through his preaching and their reception of the gospel. Paul's appeal to them is to recognize the gravity of their situation, and the value of what they have together in Christ through the reconciling power of God. He is concerned for both their common affection and their common righteousness.

2 Corinthians 6:14-7:1 | *The last section is found in 6:14 to 7:1. The long defense of the credibility of the apostolic mission, which began back at 2:14 with all its power and penetrating theology, now comes to a crescendo. Two questions can be posed: First, why does Paul end it in this manner? Second, what is the literary, historico-cultural and theological context? The ending seems to be focused on an actual situation in Corinth that needs to be addressed. I doubt that this section is addressing some general problem, which amounts to something like the Corinthians hanging out with unbelievers.*

From a literary point of view, Paul constructs these verses upon that which he has previously written, especially verses 11-13, and they should be understood on this basis. He has just reminded his readers about the importance of being reconciled to God, emphasizing that "now" was salvation time; yet in addition, he has underscored his ongoing affection for them, asking them to have open wide hearts towards him, as he does towards them.

Historico-culturally we are well aware, from numerous sources including our first Corinthians, that there was a proliferation of pagan temples in Corinth. They were literally all over the place. This seems to have been a constant threat to the believing community in the city.

Theologically, what Paul is getting at here is nothing short of radical. It is impossible, from his point of view, to consider God and idols as having anything theologically in common. There is a vast and unbridgeable asymmetry here. Idolatry, if we think more and better about it, stretches from the present to a long way back in time. This particular expression of it in Corinth is theologically, as are all the rest, a misconception of the truth of God.

The conclusion begins with the famous and much discussed verse 14a. Many believers today establish their view of relations with unbelievers or marrying an unbeliever on this verse. But before making too much out of this and ending up with a wrong-headed way of handling and interpreting the biblical text, let's look at it carefully. Paul uses a metaphor from Leviticus 19:19 concerning the cross breeding of animals and Deuteronomy. 22:10 which prohibits the yoking together of an ox and a mule for plowing. The point of this is to show there is a difference between believers and unbelievers. If this is the case, a believer is to be rightly concerned about what this might mean. It is important to recall that Paul does not forbid social contact with unbelievers (1 Cor. 5:9-10; 10:27) or staying married to one (1 Cor. 7:12-14).

What then does it mean to be yoked together with unbelievers and that believers are not to do this? The following verses, I think, put the matter in perspective.

In verses 14b-16a, there are five rhetorical questions which express an asymmetry. He begins with "for" in verse 14b and after the questions concludes with another "for" in 16b. The asymmetry is evident in each of the things that Paul writes. But what is he getting at? It seems he is targeting the problematic of participation in pagan temple activity and wanting to accentuate that believers and unbelievers are not to be related to each other at this level. The total incompatibility on this register is expressed in the climactic question of verse 16a, "what union is there between the temple of God and idols?"

In verse 16b Paul makes it clear. He again begins with "for" affirming that believers are the temple of the living God. The God of believers is not a lifeless figure who resides in a lifeless building, but a God who is animate, dwelling with his people and in their presence. Corinth, as the Rome, Zurich, New York, London, Seoul, or Sydney of today held out many opportunities for a believer to be defeated. The Corinthians are on the border line of being swallowed by their culture of idolatry.

Paul assures believers with verse 16c which makes an allusion to Leviticus 26:11-12. God has promised to live with his people, to be among them, to be their God and they will be his people. This promise, Paul agrees, is now fulfilled and should have a present impact on believers association with unbelievers concerning the cultural temples of idolatry.

This assurance is followed by a direct imperative and two more promises, which come from the Old Testament. Isaiah 52:11 had addressed Israel during their time of exile to the Babylonians. Recall that the battle was not only of succumbing to a foreign power, but also succumbing to its gods, understood as idols, rages throughout Isaiah. The command to come out and be separate touching nothing unclean now is applied to believers who are in danger of compromising their belief by participating in idolatry, specifically in this context, in the form of pagan temple activity.

The first promise comes from Ezekiel 20:34 to show that God will indeed receive his people as they separate themselves from the devastating influences of foreign gods and foreign people. The second promise is adapted from 2 Samuel 7:14 and Isaiah 43:6 and affirms that God is a father to them, a father in the best sense of that reality. Believers are his sons and daughters in that through Christ they are in new covenant community with Him.

Finally, in 7:1 we have a sensitive appeal in the form of an exhortation on the whole matter. Because of the present reality of having God's promises, believers are to, as we have it here in temple ritual language, be pure, exiled from what defiles, both in body and spirit.

The result is a moving towards being a temple that is holy, which will not take place should believers be so carried away by their cultural quasi-religious and spiritual contexts that they lose the reality of what and who they are to be in the first place. Being God's temple incites believers to a proper sense of action and being in community with God in the light of who he is, and to whom they belong.

Where does all this leave us? How are we to understand this passage for ourselves today? I hope we already have some idea of how to respond to these questions. Our actions are important. How we live as followers of the crucified and risen One is important. We are God's temple, and in some sense, a visible representation of his presence in our lives and in the world. What a privilege and what a responsibility.

What verses 14 and following have given us (if my exegesis is better than worse) is that believers should not associate with unbelievers in pagan temple activity connected to idolatry. Today, we face cultures and live in cultures saturated with idolatry in a wide diversity of forms: Alcohol, drugs, money, possessions, sex, spiritualities, and so forth. All believers should be on common ground in aiming to not participate with unbelievers, or perhaps considering our own context, with believers who indulge in such forms of idol worship. In other words, there are areas of black and white.

But there is also another level, which verses 14 and following don't give us, but that Paul has written of elsewhere. As I have said, he does not exclude social and even post-marital contact with unbelievers. Take for example the whole apostolic mission. Paul and other apostles spent massive amounts of time, as the crucified and risen One had, with unbelievers. Mission was important—certainly human beings are to be valued as human beings and not merely as missional targets—yet mission is a significant part of being a follower of Christ.

Further, believers are to engage, redeem what is bad, and embrace what is good in culture and in unbelievers' lives. On this level, there is greater flexibility and participation; contexts will differ depending on who we are. Christians have been too narrow here, and it is time to move in another direction. We are to be culturally savvy, deeply aware of who God is and who we are in Christ, and graciously sensitive, as we battle against an idolatry-saturated culture, living in an age, perhaps all the more lamentable, of Christianity lite.

.

..

...

Reflections?

Imagination | *According to Webster's Dictionary the definition of imagination is as follows: a) the act or power of forming mental images of what is not actually present, b) a foolish or unrealistic notion or idea akin to fancy, which is the mind forming images well removed from reality.*

> *"Imagining is everything – it is the preview of life's forthcoming attractions."*
> *–Albert Einstein.*

Read Psalm 97:1-7

¹*The LORD reigns, let the earth be glad;*
 let the distant shores rejoice.
²*Clouds and thick darkness surround him;*
 righteousness and justice are
 the foundation of his throne.
³*Fire goes before him*
 and consumes his foes on every side.
⁴*His lightning lights up the world;*
 the earth sees and trembles.
⁵*The mountains melt like wax*
 before the LORD,
 before the Lord of all the earth.
⁶*The heavens proclaim his righteousness,*

and all the peoples see his glory.
⁷All who worship images are put to shame,
those who boast in idols—
worship him, all you gods!

Read Isaiah 11:1-9

¹A shoot will come up from the stump of Jesse; from his roots a Branch will bear fruit. ²The Spirit of the LORD will rest on him—the Spirit of wisdom and understanding, the Spirit of counsel and power, the Spirit of knowledge and the fear of the LORD— ³and he will delight in the fear of the LORD.

He will not judge by what he sees with his eyes, or decide by what he hears with his ears; ⁴but with righteousness he will judge the needy, with justice he will give decisions for the poor of the earth. He will strike the earth with the rode of his mouth; with the breath of his lips he will slay the wicked. ⁵Righteousness will be his belt and faithfulness the sash around his waist.

⁶The wolf will live with the lamb, the leopard will lie down with the goat, the calf and the lion and the yearling together; and a little child will lead them. ⁷The cow will feed with the bear, their young will lie down together, and the lion will eat straw like the ox. ⁸The infant will play near the hole of the cobra, and the young child put his hand into the viper's nest. ⁹They will neither harm nor destroy on all my holy mountain, for the earth will be full of the knowledge of the LORD as the waters cover the sea.

Imagination is a fascinating topic of interest and debate in today's world. The deeply significant issues of the real and the unreal have never been as evident as we find them in our own cultural context. Discerning between fact and fantasy, objectivity and subjectivity, in our post-modern setting, means we have to deal with a new blurring of categories, which may threaten older precision-crafted paradigms and previously settled ways of thinking. As we increasingly find ourselves in a culture that prioritizes the visual over all else, images can tend to dominate the landscape of life. Engaging the challenges of post-modern thought, for better or worse, may now suggest that we have to reassess our understanding of God, ourselves and the world. That which has been previously assumed to be real, might call for re-exploration.

Let's face it, in the twenty-first century we're seduced by the magnetism of pseudo-reality technology, saturated in images, and coerced by subliminal messages that spike the imagination.

Does it matter that sometimes we're not even aware of what's happening, yet our imaginations have been engaged, affected, and culturally influenced in certain directions? Do we perhaps need to be alert to the possibility that our imaginations can and do provoke and affect our actions?

READING CULTURE

What are Christians to make of cultural texts and the way they impact our spirituality? *Cultural texts are human productions of ways of living in the world. Think of the vast array of films, music, TV sitcoms, and shopping spiritualities that aim to sketch out maps for us to follow concerning what life's all about. How are we to read them? Connect or disconnect? Reading and interpreting culture is massively important for being part of God's mission to the ends of the earth and for the sake of the gospel, but also for critically engaging with and learning from the ideas and messages of the poignant expressions of life in our times.*

*I'm going to make the bold claim
that shopping controls far too much
of the Christian imagination and in turn
how we view ourselves, others, and the world,
       perhaps even God.*

Do you think this assertion is too strong?

Cultural texts captivate us as they invite us into a world—but what world? Whose world? And where is this world taking us? Part of our problem is with the empty imaginations that churches tend to cultivate—"shoppers' world" may too often not only be the message of some cultural texts, but also many churches. Riding the cultural wave stands us in good stead with shopping spirituality, but when there is really no significant difference between us and the cultural texts around us, there are some radical changes that need to take place.

Lamentably, few churches are teaching Christians how to read the book of culture and the book of God so that we can understand what kinds of worlds we're dwelling in. Creative, insightful, imaginative, and wise reading strategies could be four facets of serious Christian engagement with both texts, but we face severe impoverishment as all too often the book of God—and the book of culture pale into monologues. Mission crashes and begins to fade, while our spirituality descends into flames of insignificance.

Jesus was subversive in his mission to the world. He read his culture in both a critical and a sympathetic manner.

Any suggestions on how we can do better in tearing down and building up as we follow in the footsteps of Christ?

Christian Idolatry | *I want to explore some thoughts on consumerism and a cleverly devised Christian spirituality, which really speaks more of our impoverishment, than of being in community with God. I'll begin with this observation.*

Eugene Peterson in his outstanding book Living the Resurrection, 36, has some provocative words for us on this subject:

"There are books, videos, and seminars that promise to let us in on the Christian 'secret' of whatever we feel is lacking in our life — financial security, well-behaved children, weight loss, sex, travel to holy sites, exciting worship, celebrity teachers.

It isn't long before we're standing in line to buy whatever is being offered. And because none of the purchases does what we had hoped for, or at least not for long, we're soon back to buy another, and then another. The process is addicting. We become consumers of packaged spiritualities.

*This also
is idolatry. We
never think of using
this term because
everything we're buying
and paying for is defined
by the adjective Christian.
But idolatry it is, nevertheless.
It's packaged as a product – God
depersonalized and made available as a
technique or a program. The Christian market
in idols has never been more brisk or lucrative.
The late medieval indulgences that provoked
Luther's righteous wrath are small potatoes compared
with what's going on in our evangelical backyard."*

What do you think? Has Jesus become a product? Billboards and signs for Jesus?

I guess this is an indication that for some Christians, Jesus now becomes an object of a consumer culture and is reduced to a commodity. The plight of a consumerist world view and spirituality is that it ends up sucking the life out of whatever crosses its path, as we risk falling deeper into patterns of idolatry: Self-consuming and other-consuming. Jesus won't buy it. He's not for sale.

These forms of consumer spirituality rob us of hope—the idol of consuming is merely a momentary blip—empty worship that will result in hopelessness. Buying is dead—Jesus is alive. To embrace this truth in the midst of consumerism will take courage and a willingness to be submerged in God's ways against idolatry, which promote true hope.

A Letter

Dear Greg,

I can't figure out why it's so hard for me to be happy. I miss feeling like I have something to offer. I know all this work is for the purpose of getting me to a place where I can do better work, but that is so hard to remember. I've consistently been unhappy at my workplace. I've gone to counseling and seen a spiritual director. I run, I employ all my anti-depression strategies (including medication), I live in an intentional community, but I'm unhappy there and can't figure out why. I believe part of it is feeling like my major issue is—is God good? But also, what does it mean to live as a Christian in a messy world? I'm no closer to having these questions resolved than before. Not that I necessarily assumed they'd be resolved—I just want to be able to live better—to live without so much doubt. What frightens me is that I spent so much time really pouring over these questions and I came to some good conclusions and yet I keep slipping back into them. I don't think that means that the conclusions I came to weren't good or valid, rather, I seem to have a faulty memory. I need to work on remembering what I've learned. Will you pray for me about that? I really do believe that God is present and good, but I don't live that way. I still drink too much, and sleep with the wrong people. It's more practice that I need to work on— how to live well, how to be healthy, even when I see and interact with sad or frightening things everyday.

and Response

Dear Friend,

I'll start out my response to what you've written in this way: Where would you be happy? What is happiness? In whatever we do, won't we miss not being able to be doing something else? Granted, not everyone cares, but some of us are harder to satisfy than others. I would think that you'll always have something to offer because you're you and that is true wherever you are... Life and living as a Christian don't seem to be about ready-made resolution, but persistent tension. The two questions you mention about God's goodness and living as a Christian in a messy world are somewhat unresolved for me, too. Doubt is present in my life, but it doesn't reign in my life or rule it. Slipping back into the questions will always be with us—it's inevitable if one is going to be honest—but we never start at zero, because we live on the basis of answers that are adequate. Every time I fall into severe doubt, I find there are authentic intellectual and spiritual responses that point me back to the living God and his goodness. Doubt and its power can diminish in a messy world. Ah, yes, memory and remembering. I'll pray... Living "as if" is part of living as we seek to follow in the footsteps of the crucified and risen One. If you're not living as if God is present, then you're shooting yourself in the foot, and we do that sometimes, but the redemptive power of Christ sweeps us up into deep consolation and memory becomes actuality—we can start again and learn to live better and to be redeemed in the shadow of the cross.

Depth in Spirituality | *Terry, a student in our community, mentioned this during his time here: "I'm frustrated with what is often portrayed as Christianity today. There is so much that is trite and superficial, without a care for depth and a connection between truth and love. How can we move in new directions?"*

I responded: Seems to me, you should be frustrated. The current portrayal of the Christian faith, in many circles, is not only frustrating to you, but no doubt to God, as well. From what I can tell, God doesn't appear to endorse the shallow and trivial. If that's the case, you're right to protest, seek new directions, and to want an increased credibility.

God is on your side. What is passed off as 'Christian' today often goes against the very core of what it means to follow in the footsteps of Christ – the crucified and risen One. Somehow we've lost the vision that love and truth are to go together. To move in new directions, it is imperative to understand that Christianity is about as deep as it gets.

First and foremost it's about being in community with God, through Christ, in the power of the Spirit, and being in community with others—from there we are then called to live in love on the basis of the truth of redemption and forgiveness situated in the reality that the God of Scripture exists, has created this world, and sent Christ to restore it. There's real depth here: Deep, deep love, and deep, deep truth in contrast to the trite and superficial.

Passage from John 3 | *In John 3, Nicodemus and his close followers recognized something about Jesus—"we know that you are a teacher from God" (verse 2)—yet the radical change of being born again that Jesus speaks of is inconceivable for Nicodemus and his disciples. From 2:24-25 we learn that Jesus knew what was in everyone. Surely, he knew the thoughts, schemes, and interests present in the person of Nicodemus. Remarkably, Jesus welcomes the Pharisee and his questions and comments, but challenges Nicodemus and those with him to adopt a new perspective.*

*Nicodemus,
through   this
encounter, is on his way to
believing that Jesus is more than just
a teacher from God. New birth is a spiritual
requirementoftransformation.TotrulyseeGod'srule
and to enter into it requires the new ways of
seeing and new ways of being offered
by Jesus, who has the capacity
to lead people out of
darkness and into
the   light.*

Text and Worship | *Disenchanted worship is de-textualized worship. I don't mean to say that a biblical text-based worship is the only or even the best way to engage with God, but hopefully for some of us, it results in turning our hearts and minds—the whole of our lives to God, and in so doing, bringing us to*

worship in a fresh way.
One of the central aims of worship is to encounter God, not just talk or sing about God.

In biblical text-based worship it is crucial to see ourselves as actors in God's drama of creation, salvation, and the renewal of all things—the crucified and risen One playing the key role. As we do this, Scripture and its director the Holy Spirit will refresh our memories, ignite our imaginations, and empower our hearts and minds to live out the community we have with God and each other into the world.

This means that our task is to be careful readers of Scripture as an act of worship. Doing so will lead us to follow in the footsteps of the crucified and risen One. No doubt worship comprises, but is not limited to addressing people with the gospel in love, and challenging strongholds of evil and oppression, as we live destiny-directed and destiny-oriented lives caught up in the renewal that God is bringing about in space and time.

Memories | *In our pasts, we may have experienced abuse, suffering, shame, guilt, and pain; or pride, being the center of attention, and self-sufficiency. Memories may haunt or revive us—but either of these outcomes may contribute to losing the path to the spiritual life. If we are always returning to our pasts and reliving pain or vanity, then we're following our own map, and not God's map.*

Here's the point. *We may be prone to live in and be obsessed by our pasts, before coming to Christ. We may assume that the burden or blessing of such a past is what identifies who we are in the present. If we're caught living in this past, as if it is all that we have, we're giving our pasts a much greater place in our lives than they should have.*

How do we live with our memories and what perspective are we to have toward them? What are we to do with all the wonderful or horrible things that we did to others, that were done to us, or that we did to ourselves? Are we not now the same people we were in those moments?

If we aren't careful, our present life becomes merely one of remembering. We spend a good deal of time re-viewing our unredeemed pasts. Remembering is important, but when the past dominates the present to such a degree that it potentially controls who we are, it becomes a problem. To prevent that, we are well advised to understand what role the past plays in living spirituality in the present. Otherwise, our yesterdays end up entirely identifying our today. Let me explain further.

When we are down, we try to build ourselves up by looking back to previous exploits. Remember our great high school team? We won the championship that year—we are still amazing. Or when we are up, we tear ourselves down by looking back to previous failures. Remember that broken relationship? If we failed once, we'll surely fail again. And there may even be times when we find ourselves doing a bit of both in order to avoid dealing with the present.

To move in a different direction, I suggest that we reflect on the past with a present-redemptive memory. If we are currently Christians, this means that from a redemptive perspective, the life we lived in the past identifies less and less of who we are now. Being a Christian creates a new identity for us, and from the point of conversion on, we should begin to view and deal with the past in a fresh way. To understand our identities, it is essential to understand our redemption in Christ now provides us with the primary outlook for the present. From that ever-present perspective, we are to see everything else that preceded it.

(left intentionally blank for notes)

To Christian parents,

Generally speaking, many young adults today are in a desperate struggle to hang onto their faith in Christ. The options they're being presented with in their families often act as a counter to, rather than an affirmer of, genuine faith. What's going on? Here are a few scenarios that may help explain why especially the 18-30 year olds in Christian contexts, are drifting away.

Some of you are the super-spiritual—head in the clouds— automatic-pilot types. You tell your kids, "God's going to take care of everything, just leave it all to God." Problem: This just doesn't happen. God does not make it all right in this life. There are many struggles of unanswered prayer, of suffering, and of loss. False expectations eventually turn into attempts to blackmail God, which exacerbates the difficulties.

Others of you are the hyper-orthodox types. You tell your children that you believe all the right stuff. It goes something like this: "We've got the truth, the whole truth and nothing but the truth." Not a shadow of doubt or turning—not a question without an answer for these folks. Problem: The answers given don't hold up to the serious scrutiny of the children, at least most of the time, because you haven't really thought through or asked really tough questions about your own faith.

Then, there some of you who are the legalistic types. You want to follow the law and shun anything to do with the "world" or culture. You constantly bring up the do's and don't's as if this is all that matters. Lots of dumping of guilt and shame on children takes place here, with the aim to get them to do what you want them to be doing. Problem: Legalistic parents lead those they love towards un-faith, and children are picking up on this with lightening speed.

After the "my parents told me so," begins to fray at the edges, it is barely a blink of the eye before it unravels entirely. Reactions begin to include: "None of this Christian stuff means anything to me. I have no idea why I should believe it anyway." These are just some of the responses that arise and harden into a type of cynicism that becomes ingrained, which makes it difficult to find a way through when talking to younger people.

I'm not saying you are entirely to blame or solely responsible for the current drift, but those of you who hold to any of the three scenarios above, do play a bigger part in it than you may realize.

Sincerely,

Greg

Reflections?

Tension and the Kingdom of God

If you're a Christian, you should recognize that tension is an important part of your life. Tension is positive and appropriate. The explicit theological marker for tension is the "already—not yet" character of the Kingdom of God. It has arrived, but is not yet complete. We are to live in the sufficiency of the "already" as we await the completion of the not yet of God's rule.

In this context, it is important to understand the "already" part of spirituality representing God's missional work in the world and in our own lives at the present time. In spite of the fact that everything is "not yet" resolved, we have a great hope rooted deeply in God's truth, which inspires us to share our faith and to live in community with God and his people.

God in the City | *God's new city measurements emphasize its perfection and completeness as the dwelling place of God. John continues to describe in further detail, at the very limits of human language, the reality of the Holy City (Rev. 21:15-21).*

[15] The angel who talked with me had a measuring rod of gold to measure the city, its gates, and its walls. [16] The city was laid out like a square, as long as it was wide. He measured the city with the rod and found it to be 12,000 stadia (about 2,200 kilometers) in length, and as wide and high as it was long. [17] He measured its wall and it was 144 cubits thick (about 65 meters), by man's measurement, which the angel was using. [18] The wall was made of jasper, and the city of pure gold, as pure as glass. [19] The foundation of the city walls were decorated with every kind of precious stone. The first foundation was jasper, the second sapphire, and the third chalcedony, the fourth emerald, [20] the fifth sardonyx, the sixth carnelian, the seventh chrysolite, the eigth beryl, the ninth topaz, the tenth chrysoprase, the eleventh jacinth, the twelfth amethyst. [21] The twelve gates were twelve pearls, each gate from a single pearl. The great street was of pure gold, like transparent glass.

The general picture of God's city is one of magnificence, brilliance, purity, and the assured rest of completion as all waiting is now translated into the present. In the midst of the great city there will be direct fellowship with God and the Lamb. The "not yet" will be "already." In the literal and figurative sense, blurred vision will be corrected, healed, and brought to perfection. God will dwell with his people, and they with him in everlasting community.

Fairy Tales: A New Beginning?

James Poniewozik has written an interesting piece in Time magazine: "The End of Fairy Tales? How Shrek and friends have changed children's stories."

Here's my commentary:

In the old days, says Poniewozik, fairy tales went something like this: "The good were pretty, the evil ugly, and the morals absolute." Then Shrek appeared and showed us that appearance was a masquerade and that the subtext of all that came before was flawed. Yikes! The sentimental and idealist Disneyesque portraits are now thought to be paling into irrelevance, and so much for the better, according to the opinion of some new parodyists in the monied fairy tale of Hollywood happy endings.

Applauding a new realism in today's fairy tales, Poniewozik suggests, "All this has been a welcome change from generations of hokey fairy tales with stultifying lessons: Be nice and wait for your prince; be obedient and don't stray off the path; bad people are just plain evil and deserve no mercy." Yet he has some reservations: "But palace revolutions can have their own excesses. Are the rules of fairy-tale snark becoming as rigid as the ones they overthrew? Are we losing a sense of wonder along with all the illusions?"

There's a cultural meta-text at work that makes the Shrekers willing to pay. Does it look something like this? Parody, parody, all is parody. Irony of ironies, nothing but irony makes up the tales of the new world.

How do you see it?
What's going on here,
and should we care?

Expectations of God | *I hear words like this frequently: "Well, my expectation is that God has to do this for me. You know he just has to." Perhaps, the stark, yet exquisite words penned by the famous author of Ecclesiastes, "Vanity, vanity, vanities of vanities, all is vanity" could, in our own day, be translated into, "Expectations, expectations of expectations, all is expectation." And God better meet them.*

Expectations run wild here, but they're a large part of our problem today. Okay, there's nothing wrong with expectations, unless they're playing a role they don't deserve to play. And unfortunately this is all too often the case. The Christian life, as it is sometimes portrayed, is all about ME and MY expectations being addressed and realized. Some think that being a Christian centers on "what's in it for me," not on whether or not it's true. People are getting burned by this unreality and the Christian bubble they're attempting to live in is exploding. Soon after, as it often happens, they'll start to turn away from God and perhaps attempt to seek fulfillment in: Sex, money, power, drugs or alcohol (to name a few options for escape), which in turn will only bring them worldly grief that results in death. Once they find out that this direction is as hypocritical and lacking in integrity as what they left behind, then what? They can't return to what has been shattered—selfish ambition in Christian guise—and rightly so, nor do they tend to fully embrace emptiness—equally rightly so.

But where can they turn?

Where,

if at all,

do you

see an alternative?

Misunderstanding the Holy Spirit | *In our contemporary context, with its diversity of maps and guides, there is a bewildering and powerful attraction to a make it up as we go along when it comes to the Holy Spirit. The broad availability of diverse spiritualities accompanied by the increasing levels of ambiguity and misunderstanding in our Christian circles, gives rise to a myriad of perplexing notions of spirit, which are connected to almost everything.*

There are no limits or parameters to these kinds of logic. High ambiguity is what it's all about. Whatever spirit is, it is utterly unbounded and undefined, and there is no way of identifying any of its substantial activities or core characteristics. The very thought of defining spirit is assumed to go against the nature of spirit; it is to remain vague and nebulous.

Think of expressions like, the spirit of our times or the spirit of the film. No one is quite sure what such a spirit is, but it is thought to have something to do with becoming aware of and recognizing the spirit in all things. For some this means that spirit is a concoction of new age and pagan forces focused on self-realization. Others emphasize that spirit—such as animal, river, mountain, and home spirits—make their presence felt as a sort of elusive and mystifying element that is interwoven into all things, appearing around every corner in mysterious ways. We may hear of spirit as ecstasy without argument or labyrinth without direction. Supposedly, the infinite—whatever that may be—is to be discovered everywhere. All that is finite has infinite spirit.

It is important to underscore that in such contemporary expressions of spirit we are left to our dreams and reveries, our personal opinions and feelings. So be it, many might say. Be creative. Make it up as you go along. Everyone has their own spirit and spirituality, and may define both in anyway they please.

Now let's look at this quandary. In theory, Christians acknowledge the importance of having the Bible as the map for the journey, but in practice they tend to ignore it in favor of the direct intervention and revelation of the Spirit. Personal immediacy and prompting are assumed to be more spiritual than carefully contemplating and following the map. And at what cost? In my view, the expense is spiritual impoverishment. There are an unfortunate set of similarities between some of the make it up as we go along views, and those operating in Christian circles. This should remind us of our tendency to falsely absolutize and of the need to be aware of the danger of self-deception.

—From Living Spirituality: Illuminating the Path

Mark's Prologue (1:1-13) | *This is a fascinating piece of literary artistry with clout. Take verse 1: "The beginning of the gospel of Jesus Christ."*

This seemingly banal comment is a powerhouse. In what ways?

The narrator wants readers (the Prologue contains privileged insights for readers that the characters in the story do not have) to know that something new is beginning to happen. Neither Matthew, nor Luke is self-referenced as a gospel. Consequently, Mark's narrative is embarking on a new literary adventure that is attempting to capture something of the gospel of Jesus Christ. Yet, what is new?

Note that the "of" in the gospel of Jesus Christ, immediately raises a query. Should readers take this to be suggesting that Jesus is this gospel or the proclaimer of it? This appears to be purposeful ambiguity that encourages readers not to choose between the two. Jesus Christ is both proclaimer and content of the gospel. We shouldn't always assume that ambiguity in biblical stories is negative, as it may, in fact, enhance meaning. Planned ambiguity of this sort, when it occurs, will help readers to envision truths as both/and. Jesus Christ is both proclaimer and content of the gospel, and that is something entirely and intriguingly new that gives rise to thought about God and his revelation.

Mark 1:2-3
It is written in Isaiah the prophet:
"I will send my messenger ahead of you,
who will prepare your way"—
"a voice of one calling in the desert,
'Prepare the way for the Lord,
make straight paths for him.'"

In Mark's gospel the narrator confirms the newness of what God is doing in this good news by, first of all, moving readers of the Prologue backwards in God's story—reversing the flow. In the impending drama of this story, there had been an assurance in what was already announced that this new time would arrive—the famous day, the long awaited day—when one would come to mark out the fulfillment of this promise. The time of preparing for the coming of the Lord to liberate his people was now.

The narrator selects well known OT texts that are a key to the gospel's arrival—a conflation of Malachi 3:1, Exodus 23:20 and Isaiah 40:3 appear under the heading, "As it has been written in Isaiah." The mention of Isaiah may be due to the aim of the narrator to underscore the prophetic character of three lines now converging in time.

The first line streams from the life of Israel's Exodus

and the direction received during wanderings in the wilderness/desert. The second line evokes, at the end of the OT, one who will come and judge Israel for its sinful ways. And the third line highlights, at the end of Israel's exile, that God would come to release his people. This streaming, evoking, and highlighting are configured in this potent manner to suggest that a new exodus, in the shattering of Israel's exile, is now going to happen.

The configuration of this picture sets out the development of the Prologue, but it also is of considerable importance for the unfolding of the story of the gospel of Jesus Christ and for us who follow him.

Biblical Interpretation | *Today more than ever, biblical interpreters are drawing upon the knowledge of the histories, societies, cultures, and texts of biblical times in order to understand the Bible better. One of the most prominent features of this has been our rediscovery of the importance of narrative. No doubt this has something to do with the dramatic rise of our attraction to literature and especially the significantly renewed interest in stories. Think of the fascination (for better or worse), with The Lord of the Rings, Harry Potter, and The Chronicles of Narnia – or with the music of Rhapsody and others who are telling stories through their compositions.*

> *Yet, the biblical writers were way ahead of us. Literature and stories—narratives were highly important in their times as they wrote complex and careful recountings under God's direction of something of what God was doing with and through the created world, humanity, Israel, and Jesus Christ. As we may be well aware, the Bible is a mega-story—a monumental story—told through different literary forms and styles. Participation in the story is key to living it. And living it is to recognize that you have a place in God's community and mission to the world, for the sake of Christ and the gospel.*

Destiny | *Everybody is interested in the subject of the end of the world. As any Internet search engine will show, there is an astronomical number of entries on this topic. Curiosity drives us towards seeking to understand what the future holds for ourselves and the world, and there is definitely no shortage of books, websites, or blogs that attempt to predict it for us.*

We live in a world where wars and rumors of wars proliferate, the threat of nuclear devastation and climate calamities multiply, genocide and racism flourish, and dictators dominate and destroy their people; meanwhile peace, progress, technology, and prosperity seem to steam ahead in a basically unperturbed manner.

Furthermore, today we face the risk of a financial meltdown, are plagued by a massive housing crisis, and continue to be enslaved to spiraling oil prices. For many people these pervasive tendencies are an indication that we are living in the last days. Time is running out and the denouement is at hand. How are we to respond? What is our part in the unfolding story? We desperately long to see ahead to next week, to next year, and eventually to where our final destiny lies, as the reality of death looms over us all. We all want to know if the world will ever end, and what will happen to us if it does?

The book of Revelation offers acute and compelling responses to the previous questions, as well as raising a host of others. This remarkable text contains mysterious codes, highly symbolic imagery, significant turning points in time, shifts of historical perspective, and a mixture of heavenly and earthly visions that saturate the landscape of life and death.

What might these have to do with the future of the world and our ultimate

destiny?

Revelation announces that the age-long battle between good and evil is headed for a vital showdown and that God is and will be victorious as history is brought to a close. When it all comes down, and it will, we need to know whose side we're on. This means there are many important questions to be asking ourselves including:

Who are we following?
How are we living?
And where, if anywhere, are we going?

Several years ago, someone once told me that Saddam Hussein was the antichrist and that the end of the world was at hand. There was another prediction circulating around at roughly the same time: Europe moved towards unification—the European Union was the beast. This new organization of countries was assumed to be a clear sign of the fulfillment of the end times. These sorts of preposterous predictions have side-tracked readers and not helped us better understand or live out the truth of Revelation—this relevant, frightening, and crucial part of the Scripture.

Tree of Life

(Proverbs 13:10-14)

*By insolence the heedless make strife,
but wisdom is with those who take advice.
Hope deferred makes the heart sick, but a desire
of goodness fulfilled is a tree of life. The teaching
of the wise is a fountain of life so that one might
avoid the snares of death. | Our communities are to
be trees of Life. Living trees have roots in Scripture;
trunks of solid Christian teaching, apologetics, prayer,
mission, innovative cultural insights, and hospitality;
branches that stretch out in symmetrical, yet diverse
directions; and leaves that flourish because of their
dependence on being connected to the rest
of the tree, while at the same time
bringingnourishment*

a n d

*contributing
something
vital so that the
"tree" remains
strong and living.*

And Rome Fell - Revelation 18 | *The people of the earth have committed adultery with "the harlot" by participating in ungodly activities and open rebellion against God. They stand in awe at the destruction, which came so suddenly; weeping and mourning over the loss of the supposed luxury, wealth, and power.*

"Woe! Woe! Woe!"
instead of
"Holy! Holy! Holy!"

The merchants too will weep and mourn for their loss of revenue as their market completely collapses. Much has been written about the luxurious lifestyle of Rome and the extravagances of its banquets and parties. The Romans were wealthy enough to spend massive amounts of money and the staggering volume of goods bought provided merchants with much of their income.

It is worth mentioning a few things on this list of imports to have some idea of the purchasing power of Roman society in John's day. Gold, silver, fine linen, silk, were status symbols to a Roman citizen. Many of these imports were from around the world. Africa, China, Egypt, Phoenicia and other locations all had great trade with Rome (Ezekiel 27). Along with fine textiles and precious metals, human beings were considered to be merchandise as much as any other commodity. The slave trade may have been the most profitable and prized of all, and some estimates indicate there were massive numbers of slaves in the Roman Empire.

Note that the phenomenal amount and tremendous variety of imports made Rome the center of the world and gave the city a sense of greatness, arrogance, and power. The strong belief was that Rome would never fall; its reign would never come to an end.

—From Living Apocalypse: A Revelation Reader and A Guide for the Perplexed

There may be some frightening parallels here with where we are today. Do you think the West will f$_a$

l_l

?

Poetic Spirituality / **The poetry of the Psalms addresses us as a bundle of life in community with God. While God, Psalmist and Israel wrestle, darkness hovers over the landscape of time. Light escapes, but is captured again when God graciously illumines the path ahead. In the covenantal mapping literature of the Psalms, we find powerful claims of trust and gratitude mixed with disclosures of deep despair and estrangement.**

In the Psalms, we see creational affirmations and covenant shattering, combined with a longing for a renewal of relational safety and stability. As the Psalmist might cry out, May your goodness, oh God, shine through and lament not be our lot in life. Lord, keep us by your side in the land of the living.

Living spiritually is enhanced and enriched through the Psalms and their frequent affirmations of and appeals to God's covenant loyalty. Many of these writings, however, may shock us with their realism. In the midst of our sometimes automatic pilot spirituality, where everything is supposedly bright and happy, some of the Psalms remind us that community with God and the path to life are far from straight forward.

There is and will be brokenness, mystery, dark times, judgment, desperate searching, and much more. Though these circumstances frequently lead to illumination and new understanding, arriving there means going through—not taking a detour around—facets of spirituality that may not fit our desired schemes, notions, and expectations of God. The path may become difficult and the destination may seem far away, but God is faithful to lead us forward. The Psalms are a richly textured slice of life with God, and they offer us revelatory insights into humanness and living spirituality.

Our obsession with ME subverts the truth that the death of Christ is a key event in the establishment of God's rule. Why did Christ die? Christians often respond, "He died for ME and my sins." While this is astonishingly true, there is a caveat—Christ died for far more than that. The whole of God's reign is at stake in Christ's death as he takes the covenant curses upon himself. The Kingdom of God has burst on the scene, and the death of Christ is first and foremost about inaugurating this rule. Christ's death is not about less than ME and my sins, but it is always superabundantly about so much more—God's establishing his rule and restoring all things. And that is what we miss.

When I put myself—ME—at the center, the death of Christ and living spirituality are considerably impoverished. There is a place for me, but it is important to say "no" to ME being at the center. This involves a real battle—the battle with sin. Life and death are at stake. And if we choose to center on ME, we are facing the significant danger of embracing forms of spiritual impoverishment—notably, idolatry and self-deception.

Christians are called to live otherwise: For the Other and others. We are not called to constantly focus on ourselves. The scriptural mapping speaks of loving others and serving them. It speaks of evangelism, social action, and putting others before ourselves as illuminating the true path toward living spirituality. And Christ is the prime example in that he lived and died for others.

—From Living Spirituality: Illuminating the Path

Flight From the Ordinary

The perpetual flight from the ordinary seems to capture our attention. We find ourselves, gradually, or even all of a sudden, moving away from living a truly spiritual life. Somehow there is little or no attraction to the ordinary. It fails to strike us. Maybe it's because there is less hype, flash and spin than the cultural circus of the Western church, with all its glitter and consumer strategies. What do you think? • *Focus on the ordinary. Take for example, preparing a meal, serving it to strangers and eating together. This doesn't happen often enough in our churches. Too ordinary? As one dimension of the ordinary part of daily life, this important feature of hospitality is fast disappearing, along with other tangible and practical routines of down to earth spirituality. Does it matter? Let's start here with the ordinary.* • *In his powerful book Living the Resurrection, 49-50, Eugene Peterson makes these comments in his chapter entitled "Resurrection meals."* • "'Let's get on with life' can serve as a kind of subtext for our pursuit of spiritual formation and how easily and frequently the spiritual gets disconnected from our daily lives, leaving us with empty Godtalk. It's not that Godtalk is untrue, but when it is disconnected from the ordinary behavior and conversation that make up the fabric of our lives, the truth leaks out." • "It is not an uncommon thing among us that a disconnection takes place between our

Christian identity and God, between our friends and God, between our work and God. Then there is no more life—just Godtalk. The life leaks out, and we're left flat." ▪ *Then Peterson emphasizes his point once again, 71-72.* ▪ "Christian practice in matters of spiritual formation goes badly astray when it attempts to construct or organize ways of spirituality apart from the ordinariness of life. And there is nothing more ordinary than a meal. Abstract principles—the mainstay of so much of what is provided for us in contemporary church culture—do not originate in biblical revelation." ▪ *Formation-by-resurrection, Peterson suggests, can be deeply connected to sharing a meal. He highlights the notion that such meals, because the resurrection really took place, begin to starve out self-importance and enhance a common understanding of our humanness. Sitting down at home and sharing a meal with others can be a spiritual marvel.* ▪ *Looking to the two meals at Emmaus and Galilee, where Jesus was host, creates for us a new way of sharing a meal – in Jesus' resurrected presence. Jesus extends the offer to participate, receive and engage, yet with no arm twisting, as the meal provides that which is necessary.* ▪ *To practice resurrection means an inclusion of all of what we say and do, which by and large is made up of the ordinary joys and tasks of daily life. Eat together, and share in the resurrection formation Jesus offers to all those who are hungry.*

The Shroud of Secrecy | *Did you ever notice the high level of secrets in the lives of Christians? "Keep this quiet. Don't tell anyone." Here's what I mean. This shroud of secrecy seems to be in place especially when it comes to the problems, doubts, and questions that people have with their faith. Any of these important issues, it is thought, must be safely hidden away. There are so many unanswered questions about Christian belief, but everyone pretends all is okay—no worries, so by all means keep these uncertainties secret.*

Myriads of Christians are caught in the shroud of secrecy. They're deeply struggling with their faith and are convinced they must not say anything about it. Fear, pride, or doubt may all be factors in their assumption that they have to hide and can't be honest. But let's face it, most of the time the shroud of secrecy is highly promoted by pastors, churches, parents, and friends who won't or don't understand. Who would ever dare tell them what the doubts, questions or problems are without facing a barrage of condemnation? The reality of trusting others in the Christian community has been blown apart and deeply severed.

Keeping the secret becomes more important than keeping the faith.

Right?

What happens next is that these people of the shroud drift away. Not being able to be honest about serious doubts or questions that deserve to be heard, leads them to despair. Drifting into and being covered by the shroud of secrecy, however, is a covert operation that has nothing to do with the gospel of Jesus Christ.

Everyone who finds themselves in the shroud of secrecy is to be encouraged to break through. They should be welcomed, and responded to in grace, in patience, and in love. Instead the reverse happens, they're taught to keep it all a secret. Our lack of openness here is lamentable, tragic, and perverse. As followers of the crucified and risen One, we should do all we can to tear the shroud apart. If you have the opportunity, support those with questions. God may be on their side. Give them honest answers; seek to be credible and to meet them where they are. And while you're at it, be sure to ask yourself some questions about your own faith. Let's work together to diminish the shroud of secrecy that tends to define and debilitate so many Christians.

False Absolutes | *I wonder if the old tendency to possess absolute knowledge on the basis of human reason has been exchanged for the new tendency to possess absolute humility on the basis of human feelings. I'm not sure, but it seems to me that we may have been captured by false options here.*

Do you think Christianity offers us a true one?

As those who follow the crucified and risen One, we're to grow increasingly aware that love is engraved on us, etched into the depths of our souls. Love should be the imprint that produces Christian unity and identifies us to the watching world. When people look at us, they are to see our love for each other and the unity that results from this love. - - - John 17:20-23 makes this directive abundantly clear. Our unity and community like that of the Father and Son has an impact on the world. This unity is one of the central features that make it possible for the world to know that the Father sent Jesus, and that he loves us. A scriptural mapping confirms that this is the path to life and that these are the chief characteristics by which the unbelieving world will recognize that we are in community with God and true disciples of Jesus.
- - - We have at times expressed this love and unity poorly to those that are seeking. We have been unloving by not giving honest answers to honest questions, and we have not shown enough love to our brothers and sisters in Christ in order to have unity wherever it can be

found. As disciples of the crucified and risen One, we are acting as if there is no engraving, no etching, and no imprint; we are acting as if we have not been loved by Jesus, and as if the Father has not sent the Son. Lamentably, we are missing the mark of a Christian and failing to truly love others and to be unified. This—it must be said loud and clear—is deplorable. - - - Growing numbers of Christians and non-Christians are bewildered by a sense of the inauthenticity and the lack of real and genuine love among us. The words fake, arrogant, and aloof all too often describe and characterize us, both inside and outside the Christian community.

- - - Believers become apathetic and cynical. They're floundering and drifting. Unbelievers look and say, "Who cares." There's nothing different in the Christian community. Then, these unbelieving observers turn away and go about business as usual. And all the while we are consumed with constructing our Christian bowling alleys and health clubs, dogmatically privileging our doctrines over people, constructing our apologetics without love, chasing after the making of more and more money, or performing in the theater of cool. Living love and unity gets left behind in the shadows. - - - Where is the true Christian response of costly love today? Where have we lovingly given answers to a lost culture and comforted the souls who are trapped within it? Whatever happened to welcoming the stranger, the outcast, the disenfranchised, and following the crucified and risen One in offering hope and hospitality to the other?

Looking Towards Home | *We confess that we are damaged agents; like precious and torn leaves fluttering on the winds of time. Pain, sorrow, and tragedy may beset us, and it is helpful, though not always satisfactory, to know that we are in the good company of Job, Jeremiah, and Jesus. Their plight and its expression in Scripture may help us when we desperately search for forms of speech that will give voice to our cry in the wilderness. We long to be heard, to be responded to, to be released, and to be fully redeemed.*

Prayer is sometimes like this:

Crying out to God and waiting.
Through our tears about the world,
others, and ourselves, we experience a
growing awareness that we are finite beings
grappling with the infinite God. We clamor for
what to say and how to say it, stumbling along in
faith as we know, and know deeply, that God loves us.
As we struggle, although in the midst of hope, to
seek his glorious face, he will faithfully bring us
out of exile and into the new promised Land—
a dwelling space of his presence and power.

*And here,
as his beloved children,
we find our home.*

Destinée Media

Destinée Media publishes both fiction and nonfiction and aims to bring a fresh perspective to spirituality and culture.

At Destinée Media we seek to operate by faith in God within a Biblical/Christian worldview. We hope to inspire 'culturemaking' by promoting ideas that will contribute to Christ being understood as Lord of the whole of life, which is to be marked by redemption and renewal. We are committed to reflecting carefully on vital matters for the church, academy and society, while aiming to keep a personal and intimate dimension of the Christian life in view.

We thank you for your interest in our materials and hope that you find them both relevant and challenging. Please share your thoughts with us:

www.destineemedia.com

www.ingramcontent.com/pod-product-compliance
Lightning Source LLC
Chambersburg PA
CBHW030328080526
44584CB00012B/767